D0993193

Let Heaven and Earth Unite!

by
Miriam A. Weglian
and
Stephen M. Weglian

edited by
Laurie Balbach-Taylor

**Apparitions of the Blessed Virgin Mary
and Messages from Our Lord,
Jesus Christ, to Bernardo Martinez,
Nicaraguan Visionary**

*Holy Lady of Victory, Daughter of the Father,
give us your Faith. Mother of the Son of
God, give us your Hope. Sacred Spouse of God
the Holy Spirit, give us your Charity.
And cover us with your mantle. Amen.*

edited and published for:
The Riehle Foundation *by:*
Faith Publishing Company
P.O. Box 237
Milford, Ohio 45150-0237
U.S.A.

Declaration:

Since the abolition of Cannons 1399 and 2318 of the former Canonical Code, publications about new apparitions, prophecies, miracles, etc., have been allowed to be distributed and read by the faithful without an express *imprimatur,* providing they contain nothing which contravenes faith and morals. In the case of this book, *Let Heaven and Earth Unite!,* the Church has additionally granted such permission. Regardless, the authors, editor, and publisher wish to submit to the final judgment of the Magisterium of the Church regarding any events referred to herein.

Published for The Riehle Foundation by Faith Publishing Company.

Additional copies of this book may be acquired by contacting:

For book stores: Faith Publishing Company
P.O. Box 237
Milford, OH USA 45150-0237
Phone: 1-513-576-6400
Fax: 1-513-576-0022

For individuals: The Riehle Foundation
P.O. Box 7
Milford, OH USA 45150-0007
Phone: 1-513-576-0032
Fax: 1-513-576-0022

Front cover: "Our Lady of Nicaragua, Queen of the Americas" by Raimundo Rubio.

ECCLESIASTICAL APPROVAL FOR PARTS I AND II

AVE MARIA CONCEIVED WITHOUT SIN

CHANCERY OF LEON
Apdo. 86 • Telephones (0311) 4820/6459
Leon, Nicaragua, C.A.

I hereby authorize the publication of the Story of the Apparitions of the Blessed Virgin Mary in Cuapa and the Messages given to Bernardo Martinez under the title, *Let Heaven and Earth Unite!*

May this publication help those who read it to have an encounter with Jesus Christ in the Church through the mediation of the Mother of our Lord.

Issued at Leon, on the 10th of June, 1994, Solemnity of the Sacred Heart of Jesus.

– Mons. Bosco M. Vivas Robelo
Bishop of Leon

TABLE OF CONTENTS

Endorsement vii

Dedication ix

Prologue xi

Translator's Note xiii

Forward to English Edition xv

Background 1

Part I 15
    1982 Ecclesiastical Approvals for Part I 15
    Signs of Lights 18
    The May Apparitions 21
    The June Dreams with the Blessed Virgin Mary 28
    The July Dream with the Angel 32
    The September Apparition of the Blessed Virgin
    Mary Appearing as a Child 37
    The October Apparition 40

Part II 45
    El Crucero Apparition 45
    First Message from Jesus Christ 55
    Second Message from Jesus Christ 59
    Questions on Various Topics 66
        1. Meaning of Cuapa 66
        2. Bernardo's Childhood 68
        3. Bernardo's Schooling 71
        4. Bernardo's Occupations 72
        5. Bernardo's Visits to the United States 72
        6. Acquisition of Illuminating Statue for Cuapa 73
        7. Locution from the Virgin Concerning
           Teaching Vocational Skills 78
        8. Locution Concerning Our Lady's Future
           Victory in Nicaragua 80

9. Bernardo's Explanation of Why the Blessed
   Mother Appeared as a Child 85
10. Message for President Chamorro 85
11. Message to the World 90
12. Meaning of "Make Peace!" 91
13. Meaning of "Active, Diligent, Not Passive" 92
14. Healings at Cuapa 92
15. Names of the Virgin 94
16. Title of the Angel in Dream of July 8, 1980 94
17. Biblical References 95
18. Dream with St. Joan of Arc in 1981 96
19. Sees No Angels with Blessed Mother 100
20. Problems in the Church 100
21. Heaven 100
22. Satan 101
23. Corruption in Sandinista Government 101
24. Messages of Preparation and Hope 101
25. Impending Punishments 102
26. Bernardo's Message to America 103

Epilogue—"Dreams Do Come True" 105
   Bernardo's Ordination 105
   Padre Bernardo's First Mass..107

Appendix—Selected Prayers for the Americas..............112

Endorsement

Bernardo Martinez is one of the most balanced, transparent, and obedient visionaries that I know. He is a good peasant, who shows great spirituality, according to the popular South American culture.

He possesses a clear and spontaneous vocation since childhood, but few welcomed it. Still, he was obedient and remained a rather poor and modest hermit. He was never married.

In 1980, at the age of 50, the apparitions awakened his vocation. But he was not immediately understood. After the apparitions, he was eventually accepted in a minor seminary with young boys, and he studied patiently.

After many years, he was accepted in a major seminary and was authorized to preach every Sunday. This resulted in many spiritual fruits. In 1990, I asked him several times, "When will you be ordained?" He always answered with the same patience, "When the bishop will decide." Bernardo Martinez is obedience made flesh. Finally, with more delay than Jacob for his marriage to Rachel, he was ordained a deacon on March 19, 1995, and a priest on August 20, 1995, fifteen years after the first apparition. Glory to God.

– Father René Laurentin

Dedication

This book is dedicated to St. Joseph, one of the greatest saints ever conceived and born with Original Sin, loving spouse of the Blessed Virgin Mary, vicar father of our Lord and Savior Jesus Christ, patron of the dying, protector of the Holy Catholic Church, model for the holy worker, defender of Christian spouses, and guardian of Christian families. St. Joseph, pray for all of us, especially for Christian fathers of all races, so that all of us may better mirror the image of our Heavenly Creator. St. Joseph, ask Jesus, our Redeemer and our Brother, to bestow upon us in the Americas the graces necessary "to love life, cherish life, defend life."

Prologue

THE ETERNAL MESSAGE OF GOD TO MANKIND

1. *I, the Lord, am your God. You shall not have other gods besides Me.*

2. *You shall not take the name of the Lord, your God, in vain.*

3. *Remember to keep holy the Lord's Day.*

4. *Honor your father and mother.*

5. *You shall not kill.*

6. *You shall not commit adultery.*

7. *You shall not steal.*

8. *You shall not bear false witness against your neighbor.*

9. *You shall not covet your neighbor's wife.*

10. *You shall not covet anything that belongs to your neighbor.*

– Sinai Desert c. 1250 B.C.

Translator's Note

In order to protect the authenticity and colorful language of the messages and descriptions in Bernardo's own expressions, so genuine, so personal and so full of flavor, an attempt has been made to keep editorial changes to a minimum. The reader will find that the honesty and simplicity with which Bernardo relates his experiences present our Lord, Jesus Christ, and the Blessed Virgin Mary as being concerned about her children in one of the Central American countries with the most economic, political, social, and especially spiritual problems today.

The general picture depicted by these messages and revelations is one of immense love, mercy, and hope. In the midst of difficulty and persecution, faith overcomes, the Blessed Virgin protects her children, and the Name of Jesus, our Savior, is proclaimed and defended. May God grant that these revelations from our Mother Mary and from Jesus, our Savior, stir the hearts and minds of those in authority and of all peoples to be open to faith and conversion, so as to prepare the way for the Second Coming of the Messiah!

Jesus asked His listeners, *"When the Son of Man comes, will He find faith on earth?"* (*Luke* 18:8). Let us now answer with a definite and resounding, "Yes, Lord. You will find faith, not only on this earth (myself and my people or country), but on all the world!"

– Luis Quezada

Foreword to English Edition

Our Lady of Sorrows
September 15, 1995

In 1941, Miriam was born in Managua, Nicaragua, and I in Toledo, Ohio. Our marriage took place in 1973 at Our Lady of Victory Church, located in a place called El Crucero ("The Cross"), a little village south of Managua, Nicaragua. She is bilingual in English and Spanish. Even though my knowledge of Spanish is very limited, we share an enthusiasm for the life story of Bernardo Martinez, a simple man, born on August 20, 1931, in humble origins in Cuapa, Nicaragua; a man who is blessed by God and has been honored to receive visits from the Blessed Virgin Mary, the Mother of God, and messages from Jesus Christ, our King and Savior.

Cuapa is a small town in Nicaragua having a population of approximately 5,000 people. In the early 1880s, the area in which Cuapa is now situated contained only two permanent houses and a few Indian huts. In the oral tradition of the town, a Jesuit missionary from Mexico, Father Andres Rongier, S.J., prophesied at that time that Cuapa would become known in the future because of the apparitions of the Blessed Virgin Mary that were going to happen there.

We believe each reader will be fascinated by the events that Father Bernardo relates in his book which make Father Rongier's prophecy come true. However, each reader will have to judge for oneself whether he or she believes Father Bernardo's story. From his statement to a neighbor, as a child of eight years of age, that he "already had a girlfriend," his acquisition for the chapel in Cuapa of a statue of the Blessed Mother from a nearby city as a teenager, the apparitions of the Blessed Mother in 1980 in Cuapa exhorting her children to *"make peace,"* the apparition of our Blessed Mother holding the wounded and bruised Christ Child at Our Lady of Victory Church in 1987, and his present status, completing his childhood dream, as a priest of the Roman Catholic Church, having been ordained on August 19, 1995, in Leon, Nicaragua, by Bishop Bosco Vivas Robelo, and saying his first Mass at Cuapa on August 20, 1995, the feast day of St. Bernard of Clairvaux in whose honor Father Bernardo was named, his story exudes his love, sincerity and humanity. Father Bernardo is a blessing for Nicaragua, a tool Heaven is using to reconcile the Nicaraguan people, and all of the Americas, with God and His Holy Roman Catholic Church.

Father Bernardo Martinez's story is divided into two parts. Part I relates to the 1980 apparitions in Cuapa. It is an English translation of Father Bernardo's narrative which appeared in a 1982 publication approved by Nicaraguan Bishops Pablo Antonio Vega M. and Bosco M. Vivas Robelo. The Blessed Mother calls upon us to resume the devotion to her Immaculate Heart, including the five first Saturdays, and to make peace—peace with God, peace with our neighbor, and peace with ourselves.

Part II is an edited English translation of a debriefing of Bernardo that took place in our home in McLean, Virginia, a few days before the American Presidential Inauguration on January 20, 1993. A question and answer format is used. In it, Bernardo tells about the apparition at Our Lady of Victory Church in 1987, locutions and messages since 1980, some of his childhood experiences, and his family background.

The Epilogue describes Father Bernardo's ordination on August 19, 1995, in the Cathedral in Leon, Nicaragua, and his first Mass on August 20, 1995, in the chapel in Cuapa, Nicaragua.

The Appendix is a collection of prayers, some old, some modified, and some new, that readers may find helpful in their spiritual development.

Compiling the story of Father Bernardo Martinez has been a humbling, but rewarding, endeavor. Many people have cooperated in the effort. We would be remiss if we did not mention them. First of all, we want to thank Bishop Bosco Vivas, the bishop of the Diocese of Leon in Nicaragua. Bishop Vivas was a bishop in Managua, Nicaragua, when the apparitions occurred in Cuapa. In 1982, as previously indicated, he co-approved the Spanish publication of what is now translated into English as Part I of this book. In the summer of 1994, he also approved publication of the Spanish version for Part II. Bishop Vivas has been a protector of Bernardo during Bernardo's various ordeals, and has encouraged Bernardo to continue his education as well as his discernment of his priestly vocation. Bishop Vivas ordained Bernardo as a deacon on March 18, 1995, at the Nicaraguan National Shrine of the Immaculate Conception, which is located in El Viego, Nicaragua, a little town near Leon. While Bishop Vivas has approved the Spanish text of Parts I and II, we wish to make it perfectly clear that we alone are responsible for the English translation and the various bracketed [ ] explanatory remarks that appear in Parts I and II. Most of these remarks were not contained in the Spanish version. We added them to help explain certain things to American readers which Nicaraguans would just naturally know or where the translation just standing alone without further clarification might confuse the reader.

Because Nicaragua has recently suffered through a terrible civil war, we have included a few observations concerning it, which we believe to be fully truthful, as well as reasonably balanced. We also want to expressly tell the reader that Bishop Vivas' approval, besides not extending to the accuracy of the English translation, which we, nevertheless, believe to be totally accurate, or to the substance of the explanatory information we are providing in brackets [ ], also does not encompass the Appendix. We are solely responsible for its content. We do believe, however, that, since **prayer is the ultimate answer** to the current problems the world is facing, you will find the prayers helpful and rewarding in your private devotional practice.

Next, we thank Mr. Anthony Braddock for the interest he has shown in the Cuapa apparitions and the assistance that he has provided the Catholic Church in Nicaragua. Through Tony's efforts, Bernardo was brought to Washington, D.C., in January 1993, where he spoke at many churches in the area to help spread the messages of Our Lady of Cuapa. Many people who are not familiar with these apparitions have been very impressed with the need for peace and togetherness that Bernardo is echoing through Our Lady's words.

During Bernardo's 1993 visit, the material found in Part II was acquired. Assisting us in the taped interview of Bernardo were Mr. Joseph Cassano, a resident of Springfield, Virginia, who met Bernardo during a pilgrimage to Nicaragua in September 1992, and Miss Marlene Marenco, our niece who was visiting us from San Jose, Costa Rica. (Joe was also extremely helpful in the editing of the English transcript.) After the interview, the tapes were transcribed by Miss Esperanza Duarte, Mrs. Leila Saborio de Martinez and Miriam. Mr. Luis Quezada has been generous with his time in editing the materials and translating the original Spanish material into English. The cover, which is an original painting by Mr. Raimundo Rubio, which we have entitled "Our Lady of Nicaragua," was based upon Raimundo's conversation with Father Bernardo. Our gracious thanks to all these wonderful, talented and dedicated people, and to all the others who assisted us, but who have not been mentioned.

Lastly, but certainly not the least, we would like to thank Father Bernardo for sharing a portion of his experiences with us so that we can learn from them. We live in apocalyptic times. Major changes are occurring all over the world. Many of the faithful are heeding the calls from Heaven and are returning to the sacraments and to praying the Rosary daily. Unfortunately, many others, especially the youth, are turning to violence, sexual immorality, drug addiction, abortion, euthanasia, to name but a few. But most disturbing is the diabolic attack upon the family, the basic unit of our society. Its degradation by the "politically correct" has caused millions of divorces and instances of child and/or spousal abuse and/or neglect. The devil is all so cunning and ready to break up the natural bonds of society. Yet darkness will not be victorious. It was at Fatima that Our Lady said, *"In the end my Immaculate Heart will triumph."* Mother Mary comes now to point us in the direction of her Son, the Eternal Word, Who is the Way, the Truth, the Life, the Light, and our Hope.

Peace be with you!

– Miriam and Stephen Weglian
McLean, Virginia, U.S.A.

Background

The following article was prepared by Stephen. He is solely responsible for its contents. It is intended to help those readers who have little familiarity with Nicaragua to better understand its history and past relationships with the United States.

NICARAGUA AND THE UNITED STATES—THE PAST 150 YEARS

Nicaragua is located near the middle of Central America. Its geographical area is 49,579 square miles—almost exactly the same size as the State of New York, which has 49,576 square miles. Nicaragua's population has not been accurately counted since its most recent civil war, but it is estimated that the current population is between 3.5 and 4 million. (New York, on the other hand, has a population of over 17 million.) Most of the population of Nicaragua inhabits its Pacific coastal region. It is bordered on the North by Honduras, on the south by Costa Rica, on the east by the Caribbean Sea (Atlantic Ocean), and on the west by the Pacific Ocean. On its western coast, it is traversed by a mountain range, which is part of the continental axis for North and South America, stretching from Alaska to Tierra del Fuego, the southern tip of South America.

One of the most strategic geographical aspects of Nicaragua is that it contains the lowest gap above sea level in the entire intercontinental mountain range. More importantly, this gap occurs at a point where there would be less than forty miles of land between Lake Nicaragua and the Pacific Ocean. Because Lake Nicaragua empties into the Atlantic Ocean, there has been a dream for a long time of building a canal through this gap. Unfortunately, the gap contains an earthquake fault, as well as several active volcanoes nearby. The science of the late nineteenth century did not permit the tech-

1

nical means to cut the gap properly, and, hence, a location, which is now in Panama, was selected by the United States to build the canal linking the Atlantic with the Pacific. Lake Nicaragua is one of the biggest fresh water lakes south of the Great Lakes and north of Peru. Lake Nicaragua is also somewhat unique because it contains the only fresh water sharks that are known.

Nicaragua has very fertile land and its chief products are agricultural. Nicaragua has many volcanoes and a major earthquake fault runs through it. In December 1972, a major quake killed over 10,000 people in Managua and completely devastated its downtown portion. The Caribbean Coast is mainly uninhabitable swamp and jungle. The Mosquito Indians occupy portions of it. The Caribbean Coast was discovered by Christopher Columbus during one of his voyages to the New World in 1502. Nicaragua was part of Spain's captain-generalcy of Guatemala until it declared its independence from Spain in 1821. Its "Fourth of July" is September 15.

Historically, it is primarily a Roman Catholic country. However, in recent years, charismatic, evangelical Protestant sects have gained in numbers. As a general rule, Nicaraguans, especially the poor, show great piety, common sense, and extreme cleverness. They are hard workers when they *have* to work. They do enjoy life, however, and unlike many Americans, they do not live just to work or consume. Most Americans who have had any extended contact with the country will admit that Nicaraguans are some of the nicest people you could ever meet. They love to talk, joke, and socialize. Ruben Dario, considered one of the best poets in Spanish literature, was a Nicaraguan. When one drives throughout the country, one always sees the Nicaraguan people talking, laughing, and smiling.

Nicaragua is a poor country when measured in terms of individual annual income. Its poverty has been compared to Haiti's. These economic figures can be misleading, however, because the richness of Nicaragua is in its lands, which are extremely fertile, and, assuming they receive normal rainfall, there is an abundance of food. Nicaraguan beef, especially before the serious fighting in the civil war in the mid-1970s, is one of the best tasting in the world.

Their coffee crop can also be of superb quality. Most of the people may be poor, but they are not starving, especially since relative peace prevails now throughout most of the country.

A unique relationship has existed between the United States and Nicaragua over the last 150 years. As part of the United States' Monroe Doctrine to keep European powers outside the internal affairs of the newly independent nations in the Americas, the United States has had much contact with Nicaragua. In the mid-nineteenth century the British tried to encourage the Mosquito Indians, who inhabit the eastern Caribbean coastal regions, to separate from Nicaragua. The United States intervened diplomatically on Nicaragua's behalf, not primarily to save this land for Nicaragua, but to keep the British from establishing more of a foothold on the North American continent. (By that time the British had managed to acquire what was then called British Honduras. Since its independence in 1981, it is now called Belize. But British troops remained in Belize after it gained independence to guard against Guatemala which also claims that territory.)

In the late 1850s, a rather unique American, William Walker, was actually elected President of Nicaragua. Walker, whose name is anathema in Central America, was a "filibuster" who led a group of 58 adventurous Americans ("The Immortals") from San Francisco to fight on the side of the Leon faction in a civil war going on in Nicaragua. Leon is a major city in northwestern Nicaragua near the Pacific coast. Leon's prime enemy was the city of Granada, an older, more aristocratic city, which was located on the northwest shore of Lake Nicaragua. (In fact, it was the constant political struggle between Leon and Granada that ultimately resulted in Managua, then a small town situated between these two contesting cities, to be declared the capital. Managua, which lacks the historical architecture that both Leon and Granada possess, has since become the biggest and most important city in Nicaragua.)

Granada was a very lovely Spanish colonial city. While in Walker's time all Nicaraguan women were reported to be attractive, the women of Granada were said to be exceptionally beautiful. Perhaps for that reason, Walker switched sides and joined the Granada forces. When neither side could win the struggle militarily, a political compromise was reached with Walker becoming the elected President of Nicaragua.

During this same time period, the slave holders in the Southern States of the United States realized that the expansion of slavery into more of what is now the contiguous part of the United States seemed unlikely. They started looking for other possible places to expand slavery that bordered the Caribbean Sea. By this time, slavery within Nicaragua had already been abolished. Walker, while no fan of slavery, realized that he needed outside financial support to maintain his precarious position in Nicaragua, as the neighboring countries of Honduras and Costa Rica, as well as the still upset factions in Leon, were planning to join together to drive Walker out of Nicaragua. In an attempt to entice Southern slave money, Walker reinstituted slavery in Nicaragua, costing him his popularity, especially among the poorer classes. But his expectations were not achieved because the Southern money did not come pouring in as he had hoped, probably because the Southern investors became more concerned about the impending civil war about to start in the United States.

As he anticipated though, the forces of Honduras, Costa Rica, and Leon joined together to attack him. While these forces won many battles, they did not actually defeat Walker. With his defeat likely, Walker accepted surrendering to the United States Navy which extracted him from Nicaragua. This was acceptable to forces aligned against Walker as it prevented further bloodshed. Upon his return to the United States, William Walker was treated as a national hero in some corners, to the consternation of the White House. In fact, some newspaper articles suggest that even in northern New York City Walker was given the equivalent of what became the twentieth century's ticker-tape parade.

During the California gold rush which started in 1849, Nicaragua provided the fastest method of travel from the East Coast in the United States to San Francisco. Travelers would sail to Greytown, Nicaragua, on the Caribbean Coast at the mouth of the San Juan de Sur River. They would board a smaller craft and take it up the San Juan de Sur River and across Lake Nicaragua. They would cross the last twenty or so miles by horse or carriage to the port on the Pacific, and catch a ship to San Francisco. Competition between the Nicaraguan route and the route through what is now Panama (then part of Colombia) was fierce, with the Nicaraguan route's big selling point being that it was one day faster than the other route. (So much for the good old, slow times of the past!) Of course, both of these routes had mosquitoes (the insect) to contest with, but the mosquitoes were apparently not much competition, and these two routes were much safer and faster than crossing the American plains in a covered wagon, fighting the weather and the local American Indians.

The possibility of building a canal in Nicaragua to get from the Atlantic to the Pacific has intrigued American foreign policy makers from the 1840s. Finally in 1916, Nicaragua and the United States concluded the Bryan-Chamorro treaty which gave the United States sole rights to build such a canal. This treaty was not mutually terminated until 1970. Recently, a consortium of the world's major private shipping lines from Japan and Europe have announced plans to build an alternative to the Panama Canal in Nicaragua. If this actually occurred, and it caught the present Nicaraguan Government by surprise, it could be the economic shot in the arm that Nicaragua so desperately needs to bring it into the twenty-first century.

In 1913, in true keeping with the United States' "Good Neighbor" policy, the U.S. Marines were sent to Nicaragua to help quell civil unrest. Some Marines stayed until 1925 when they were withdrawn. The Marines were not gone long, however, before the fighting erupted again. So the U.S. Marines returned to Nicaragua in 1926 to help fight a revolutionary (or bandit, depending on whom you listen to), named Cesar Agusto Sandino. The Marines never captured or subdued Sandino, but they kept him way up in the mountains in Northern Nicaragua where he could inflict little real damage. In 1933, the United States accepted a "reform" colonel, Anastasio Somoza, who came from the small town of San Marcos, Nicaragua, to become head of the Nicaraguan military. Within a short time, Sandino accepted a truce offered by Somoza. Allegedly, Sandino was on his way to meet with Somoza, but he never arrived and has never been seen again. Within a short time, Somoza overthrew the civilian government.

The Somozas (the father and his two sons, Luis and Anastasio, Jr.) ruled Nicaragua until 1979 when the Somozas were overthrown by a revolutionary force, headed by the Sandinistas, a pro-Cuban, Marxist revolutionary group formed in the 1960s which took the name of a prior Nicaraguan "hero." The Somozas maintained a close relationship with the Government of the United States throughout their rule. The infamous "Bay of Pigs" invasion of Cuba to oust Fidel Castro during the Kennedy Administration was staged from Nicaragua, among other locations.

Pedro Joaquin Chamorro was the publisher of *La Prensa,* the most prestigious newspaper in Nicaragua. He was a national hero throughout Nicaragua for opposing the suppression and corruption in the Somoza regime. When he was assassinated in the mid-1970s, it was thought at first that his death was the responsibility of the Somoza regime. However, subsequent revelations now make it appear more likely that a faction of the Sandinistas was behind the assassination. Many believe the assassination of Chamorro was the blow that fatally wounded the Somoza regime because world leaders turned against the Somoza government shortly thereafter. Anastasio Somoza, Jr., found it difficult to obtain resources to fight the Sandinistas. Moreover, it became apparent to more and more Nicaraguans that Somoza had to go. Unfortunately, the United States, while fully aware of this situation, had a split in the White House's National Security Council on what to do and failed to develop a democratic successor to Somoza.

But the Carter Administration should not be fully faulted for failure to come up with a possible replacement for Somoza, except to say that they looked for the Nicaraguans with whom they were dealing to reach a consensus on a replacement. That, however, was a fatal error. There is a well known story among Nicaraguans that basically describes this feature of their national character to a "T." While there can be more embellished versions, the story goes like this. A group of twelve Nicaraguans are locked in a room. They will not be released from the room until they reach agreement on a new political party to save the nation. Observers outside the room hear shouting, yelling, screaming, furniture being tossed about, etc. After three weeks, they signal they have reached a unanimous agreement. The door opens, they come out hugging and kissing each other. Then their spokesperson steps forward to announce their unanimous agreement. They smile, raise their hands in victory. The spokesperson announces they have agreed to form twelve new political parties!

While the career Foreign Service officers were reporting the need to find a replacement, there were political appointees in President Jimmy Carter's State Department who were ideologically at least in tune or sympathetic with the leftist overtones the Sandinistas were espousing. On the other side, Somoza, a West Point graduate whose wife was an American citizen, had strong supporters in the U.S. Congress, who threatened blockage of several key programs crucial to the Carter Administration if the White House "did in" Somoza. Somoza, himself, was no back country politician. If he had been born in the United States, there is a good chance that he would have risen high on the political ladder. He appeared live on the *McNeil-Lehrer News Hour* on several occasions. Somoza could be a charming fellow when it served his purposes. Robert McNeil and Jim Lehrer, two of the finest TV reporters of the time, are very sharp people. They were, however, no match for Somoza. Somoza, not being the only politician in history that could bamboozle and dazzle one with words, spun circles around the usually well briefed and quick minded McNeil and Lehrer.

Eventually, but too late to spare Nicaragua the impending disaster, Somoza saw the handwriting on the wall. It occurred shortly after Somoza, or perhaps some other high official in his regime, ordered the small air force of the Nicaraguan National Guard to bomb/strafe the portion of Leon held by a relatively small number of rebels, instead of actually sending in the National Guard troops to rescue hostages and kill the revolutionaries if they did not surrender. By choosing to bomb the civilians caught in the cross fire, the last feelings of any good will among the Nicaraguan people for Somoza's continuation in power evaporated. When Somoza prepared to leave from his private airstrip at his "beach" place, Montilemar (which is now a famous international resort), the coffins of his deceased father, Anastasio, Sr., and his brother, Luis, who had been assassinated, were loaded onto the plane which was headed for Miami, after the United States belatedly promised him a safe exile.

Somoza was only in Florida for a short time when he received a telephone call from an official in the U.S. State Department. (The recollection of the parties to this conversation differ dramatically.) The purpose of the phone call was to seek Somoza's assistance in getting his successor, the former Vice-President (Urcuyo Malianos) to do something that the United States wanted Malianos to do. Somoza begged off saying he was no longer the president of Nicaragua and he could not tell the Nicaraguan President (Malianos) to do it. The State Department official insisted and said something like "that which had been given (political asylum) could be taken away." The conversation ended. Somoza, being the astute fellow that he was, understood the implication. He immediately ordered his plane to get ready and he departed the United States within hours. Somoza eventually settled in Paraguay where several years later he was assassinated. Subsequent investigations have shown that the Sandinista hit squad utilized to kill Somoza were also, or at least parts of them, involved in an earlier failed attempt to kill Eden Pastora, a rebel also trying to overthrow Somoza.

When Somoza eventually left Nicaragua in 1979 there was no other organized group to take charge except the Sandinistas. The Sandinistas, although admired for their courage in opposing the dictator Somoza, represented politically less than ten percent of the Nicaraguan people. The Sandinistas formed a coalition government, which included for a while Mrs. Violeta Chamorro, the widow of Pedro Joaquin Chamorro. The Sandinistas took the ministries controlling the military, law enforcement, and other crucial functions. Those members representing truly democratic principles, however, either left or were driven out from the coalition government by 1981 by the hard core Marxists in the Sandinista

Party. One of the other rebel leaders who was initially part of the coalition was Eden Pastora, the famous Comandante Zero. Pastora lead the southern front against Somoza along the border with Costa Rica. While certainly a socialist, Pastora was not a Marxist, and, although the most popular of the rebels with the Nicaraguan populace because of his daring raids against the Somoza Government, he was never part of the inner circle of the Sandinistas. As noted earlier, during the civil war with Somoza, an assassination attempt was made on Pastora, at first believed to be by the Somocistas, but currently the odds favor the inner circle of the Sandinistas.

The Sandinistas were a mixed bag, but at their center were hard core Marxists who were extremely pro-Castro. Initially, the United States, in the Carter Administration and the early part of the Reagan Administration, supported the Sandinista Government. As its leftist and Marxist tendencies became more pronounced, the United States ceased support and commenced funding, in various manners, the "Contras" (i.e., the name given by the American press to those opposed to the Sandinista Government).

The Contras were a mixed bag also. Most of the actual fighters were young peasants or former privates from Somoza's National Guard. While a large number of their officers were former officers in the Nicaraguan National Guard, it would be unfair to say they were ardent Somosistas. They were professional soldiers. (In Nicaragua today, the army, which until recently was still under the direct control of the Sandinista Party, albeit that Party no longer "ruled" the country, has many young professional military officers trained to fight for their country. It should not be assumed that this young officer cadre are purely political Sandinistas. They are more "soldier" than "politician.") Nevertheless, the liberal press in the United States was successful in painting the Contras as former Somocistas trying to regain their "fiefdom." Such a description helped confuse and bewilder the American public as to just who was who in Nicaragua and for what exactly they were fighting. When Congressional support for the Contras finally dried up, President Reagan's Administration sought other methods of financing the troops it had recruited and which has been placed in jeopardy by the Congressional abandonment for any funding for "offense" purposes on the field of battle. These "creative" financing efforts gave rise to the Iran-Contra scandal which produced such "folk heroes" or villains ("I don't vote for felons" became a popular bumper sticker in a recent election for U.S. Senator in Virginia) as "Ollie" North, who lost a recent election but quickly is becoming a wealthy radio commentator. The Contras never defeated the Sandinistas, and slowly, so slowly, their forces dwindled.

The attempted indoctrination of the Nicaraguan youth by the Sandinistas during their decade of power was intense and manifested itself in many areas. Math text books, for example, were even rewritten to inculcate animosity toward the Americans, who the Sandinistas always thought would once again "send the Marines." They used word problems such as:

> If during a week you killed two gringos (i.e., North Americans) on Monday and three on Wednesday, how many gringos had you killed that week?

That is but one of the efforts by the Sandinistas to instill class hatred where before little hatred existed. Nicaraguans, while poor, were never, as a general rule, resentful or extremely jealous of the rich. In fact, the rich may have been more contemptuous of the poor than the poor were of them. Sandinistas tried hard to create class hatred. Whether they succeeded, only time will tell.

The Nicaraguan mentality, however, is too independent to be dominated for a long period of time by such crude, blatant propaganda. Even if the Sandinistas failed to instill class hatred, they did a fairly good job of bringing down the rich and the middle classes and driving them into exile. Some people suspect that this dispersal has been a punishment of the Lord for the rich's prior indifference to the poor. One of the reasons that Americans and other Westerners of good will fall in love with the Nicaraguan poor is that the poor are naturally happy despite the economic poverty that surrounds them. The poor are truly grateful for whatever assistance you furnish them; their smiles tell it all. Back home, Americans are used to receiving frowns for their giving to the "poor" as if it was too little, or that they were "entitled" to more. In Nicaragua, unlike some more advanced cultures, the poor, with few exceptions, are willing to work if the economy produces the opportunities.

The destruction of the middle class in Nicaragua, which was growing prior to the massive earthquake in 1972, was hastened by the greed of the Somosistas in trying to immediately recoup, at the expense of all others, the losses they suffered as a result of the 1972 earthquake. They did this by taking unfair advantage of non-Somosista business people as well as by diverting to themselves most of the massive amount of the relief assistance that flowed in from the international community after the earthquake. Their conduct doomed the Somoza Government because it started a contraction of the middle class. (There could be a message here for America's own economic policies which are producing, in the eyes of many, the same shrinking of the middle class.) However, what the Somosistas started, the Sandinistas carried out with relish as they destroyed the entire economy of Nicaragua in their attempt to remake the Nicaraguan people in the Sandinista's own image.

But in February 1990 a miracle occurred. The Nicaraguan people voted the Sandinistas out of power and elected Mrs. Violeta Chamorro, the widow of a famous publisher, Pedro Joaquin Chamorro, whose family (Chamorro) had held influential positions in Nicaragua's history. As of this writing, Mrs. Chamorro is still President. While her faction in the government has drifted closer to the remaining Sandinista leadership, the overall power of the Sandinista Party continues to wane, probably because most Nicaraguans have seen the collapse of the former Soviet Union and the former Communist countries of Eastern Europe, as well as the "basket" condition in Cuba, and have realized that Marxism is not the answer.

When Violeta Barrios de Chamorro was elected President of Nicaragua on February 25, 1990, it was a stunning defeat to the Sandinista leadership and a shock to most of the world's press. Two interesting stories concerning the election have emerged. The first deals with the actual percentage of votes the Sandinista candidates received. The official results say they got nearly forty percent. However, some people do not believe that they received much more than ten percent of the actual vote. There is a story circulating, whether it is true or not is not known, but it is an example of good Nicaraguan humor. It seems the Sandinistas appointed one of their members to be in charge of each voting unit. In one unit near Jinotega in northern Nicaragua, when the votes were counted, the Sandinistas got zero votes. They called in their poll watcher. He admitted he did not vote for the Sandinista candidate but for another. He did so, he quickly advised, in order to make the election look fair as everyone knew the Sandinistas were going to get eighty percent or so of the vote.

The other story, which is factually true, involves a group of charismatic Christians, many of whom returned to Nicaragua to work in the Chamorro campaign before the election. Each week they would meet to pray. In the beginning, they asked for a sign from God to show that their prayers for the removal of the Sandinistas from power were being heard. They never saw a sign however. During the campaign, Nicaraguan President Daniel Ortega took off his Sandinista military uniform and campaigned in sport shirts and blue jeans. Ortega hired rock bands to entertain youths all over the country at his political rallies. He had his picture posted all over Nicaragua. The posters, containing a smiling Ortega, told the voters to vote for **Daniel**, #**5**, (fifth spot) on the ballot, on February **25**.

When the results started coming in on Sunday night, the Sandinistas, who had large political parties planned, went into a deep state of shock and despair. They could not believe it! The charismatic Christians, on the other hand, were elated. They could not believe it either! It had been a miracle. A few days later the charismatics remembered they had asked God for a sign and they never recognized one. Then it hit one of them to check out what ***Daniel* 5:25** says in the Bible. It reads:

This is the writing [of the hand on the wall] *that was inscribed:* **MENE, TEKEL, and PERES.** *These words mean:*

They were flabbergasted. *Daniel* 5:26-28 continues:

MENE, *God has numbered your kingdom and put an end to it (26);* **TEKEL,** *you have been weighed on the scales and found wanting (27);* **PERES,** *your kingdom has been divided and given to the Medes and Persians (28).*

The charismatics praised God. God had given them a sign throughout all of Nicaragua and had gotten Daniel Ortega to pay for it!

As the years have progressed, the Chamorro Government has shown that it had unfortunately inherited a trait very common to almost all previous governments in Nicaragua, namely significant corruption and gross nepotism. In all fairness, however, it must be pointed out that Mrs. Chamorro chose as part of her "reconciliation plan" to leave a considerable number of Sandinistas in key ministries of her government. While some have been removed, others still remain. Any promises made by those remaining have to be taken with a grain of salt when one realizes that these Sandinistas, who seized power to liberate the poor in Nicaragua, have still failed to vacate the residences that they took over after the revolution. It is especially sad to see that several new members of Chamorro's government were likewise found living in seized residences, most of which residences were not taken from hard core Somosistas or their active supporters.

Nevertheless, the overall signs are good for Nicaragua. Mrs. Chamorro, although a weak President in the eyes of many, has been a tool to provide a breathing period for Nicaragua to heal. Her policy of "reconciliation," even if she, herself, does not go down favorably in Nicaraguan history, just may have given Nicaragua a chance. The Sandinista Party continues to contract; business activity is gradually increasing; and, most important, the people have a sense of confidence in the future. Hope is alive in Nicaragua.

1. Statue of the Blessed Virgin Mary which illuminated in April 1980 in the old chapel at Cuapa, Nicaragua. This is the statue which had been acquired for the people of Cuapa by Bernardo Martinez when he was a teenager in the 1940s. (Taken 9/92; Photograph courtesy of Joseph Cassano.)

2. Bernardo Martinez at the site of the 1980 apparitions at Cuapa, Nicaragua. (Taken 6/94.)
(Unless otherwise noted, all photos were taken by Stephen Weglian.)

3. Bernardo Martinez in front of the grotto which has been built at site of the 1980 apparitions in Cuapa, Nicaragua. (Taken 6/94.)

4. Bernardo Martinez at the location in Cuapa, Nicaragua, where the Blessed Virgin Mary rebuked him on May 16, 1980, for not disclosing her Cuapa message. (Taken 6/94.)

5. Old Chapel at Cuapa, Nicaragua, where the statue of the blessed Virgin Mary first illuminated in April 1980. (Taken 6/94.)

6. Inside old chapel at Cuapa, Nicaragua. Bernardo Martinez is standing at the location where the statue of the Blessed Virgin Mary that illuminated was located in April 1980. Accompanying him are several members of a pilgrimage from the Diocese of Arlington, Virginia. (Taken 9/92; Photograph courtesy of Joseph Cassano.)

7. Inside the new chapel at Cuapa, Nicaragua. Statue of the Blessed Virgin Mary which illuminated in April 1980 is on the left side. (Taken 9/92; Photograph courtesy of Joseph Cassano.)

8. Bernardo Martinez in front of his former home in Cuapa, Nicaragua. (Taken 6/94.)

9. Our Lady of Victory Church at El Crucero, Nicaragua, where the Blessed Virgin Mary appeared to Bernardo Martinez on March 8, 1987. (Taken 6/94.)

10. Apparition room at Our Lady of Victory Church in El Crucero, Nicaragua. Accompanying Bernardo Martinez are several members of a pilgrimage from the Diocese of Arlington, Virginia. (Taken 9/92; Photograph courtesy of Joseph Cassano.)

11. The altar which has been constructed in the apparition room at our Lady of Victory Church, El Crucero, Nicaragua. (Taken 9/92; Photograph courtesy of Joseph Cassano.)

12. Bernardo Martinez being interviewed in McLean, Virginia, for Part II of this book. (Taken 1/93.)

13. Statue of Our Lady of Victory at Our Lady of Victory Church, El Crucero, Nicaragua. (Taken 6/94.)

14. Bernardo Martinez with his statue of Our Lady of Cuapa which was carved from the tree over which the Blessed Virgin Mary appeared in 1980 in Cuapa, Nicaragua. (Taken 1/93.)

15. Another statue of Our Lady of Cuapa also carved from the tree over which the Blessed Virgin Mary appeared in 1980 in Cuapa, Nicaragua. This particular statue belongs to Sister Paula Hildalgo, a Nicaraguan nun active in several Nicaraguan orphanages and a close friend of Bernardo Martinez. This statue has been shown to the Holy Father, Pope John Paul II. A total of four statues of Our Lady of Cuapa were carved from the tree over which the Blessed Virgin Mary appeared in 1980 in Cuapa. (Taken 9/92; Photograph courtesy of Joseph Cassano.)

16. Statue of the Blessed Mother in the Basilica of the Assumption with message to Bernardo at his ordination on August 19, 1995, in the Cathedral in Leon, Nicaragua. (Taken 8/95; Photograph courtesy of Miriam Weglian.)

17. Bernardo in front of the altar at the beginning of his ordination ceremony. (Taken 8/95; Photograph courtesy of Joseph Cassano.)

18. Bernardo prostrate before the altar during his ordination ceremony. (Taken 8/95; Photograph courtesy of Miriam Weglian.)

19. Padre Bernardo making a few remarks after the completion of his ordination ceremony. (Taken 8/95; Photograph courtesy of Miriam Weglian.)

20. Padre Bernardo distributing Holy Eucharist during his first Mass on August 20, 1995, in Cuapa, Nicaragua. (Taken 8/95; Photograph courtesy of Miriam Weglian.)

21. Bernardo being blessed by Bishop Bosco Vivas and other clergy during his ordination ceremony. (Taken 8/95; Photograph courtesy of Joseph Cassano.)

22. Padre Bernardo with Miriam Weglian and some other supporters from the United States, after Padre Bernardo's first Mass at Cuapa, Nicaragua. (Taken 8/95; Photograph courtesy of Joseph Cassano, who is on the far right.)

PART I

The Story of the Apparitions of the Blessed Virgin Mary in Cuapa, Nicaragua, in 1980

1982 ECCLESIASTICAL APPROVALS

ARCHDIOCESE OF MANAGUA

Vicar General

I, the undersigned, Auxiliary Bishop and Vicar General of the Archdiocese of Managua, authorize the publication of the narration of the apparitions of the Blessed Virgin Mary in Cuapa.

—Mons. Bosco M. Vivas Robelo
Auxiliary Bishop and
Vicar General of Managua

Introduction by Bishop Pablo Antonio Vega M.

Cuapa is a small valley, located in the Municipality of Juigalpa, in Chontales. Its inhabitants are the proprietors of small cattle ranches. It is a tranquil place with little hills typical of the region of Chontales.

> [Chontales is one of the 16 Departments into which Nicaragua is geographically divided. A Department is similar to that of a county within a state in the United States except that a Department would be substantially larger in area than a normal U.S. county. Chontales, itself, is the seventh largest Department in Nicaragua. It lies east of the capital city, Managua, and borders the north and east shorelines of Lake Nicaragua, one of the biggest fresh water lakes south of the Great Lakes and north of Peru.]

It has been nearly three years now since one of the peasants from the area arrived communicating a message which he said he received from Mary in a series of dreams and apparitions.

To discern the truth of these acts depends more on the extraordinary signs from God than the simple analysis of the events.

There have been circulated, nonetheless, versions that misrepresent the events and that distort the contents of the message. For that reason, because of the duty and the obligation to protect the wholesome piety of the faithful and for the truth of those events, in my capacity as Bishop of the area, I find an obligation to assure the authenticity of the events in order to be able to assist in discerning the true value of the alluded to message.

With this purpose in mind, I sought the collaboration of some individuals in order to gather with the greatest accuracy possible and from the personal testimony of the one who saw the visions, a report of the events, without omitting the adjunct testimony that could conform the verbally reported events.

In the first place, it is our intent to clarify the contents of the message in order to be able to establish its concordance with the evangelical message, that as a Church, we are obliged to publicly acclaim and develop to its full force and plenitude.

The "report" that we present retains the accurate content and language used by the individual who received the visions.

For our part, we are surprised at the emphasis that is given to the responsibilities that weigh on man in his duty to *"make peace"* and to "construct the world," a religious emphasis that is not typical of popular religion, which more than likely leaves it all up to God.

We hope the report which we present will serve as an invitation to reflect on the social obligations that very often are largely forgotten by any of our Christians.

Juigalpa, November 13, 1982
Mons. Pablo Antonio Vega M.,
Prelate Bishop of Juigalpa

[Bishop Vega is now retired. Shortly after approving the publication of this narrative by Bernardo concerning the Cuapa apparitions in November 1982, Bishop Vega had to flee Nicaragua because of Sandinistas, who had successfully taken control of the Nicaraguan Government after the fall of the Somoza regime. (By this time, Bernardo, himself, had taken refugee in the Minor Seminary of Managua, Nicaragua, where he was under the constant protection of the Church.) A Sandinista helicopter flew Bishop Vega to the border with Honduras with only the clothes on his back. The Sandinistas warned him not to come back. He remained in exile in the United States over the next eight years.]

Signs of Lights

**In the name of the Father,
and of the Son,
and of the Holy Spirit,
Amen.**

**I, Bernardo Martinez, am going to tell my
Bishop, Mons. Pablo Antonio Vega, of the events
in the Valley of Cuapa. I want to obey him. In
everything I submit myself to him.**

It was in the old chapel that the signs began, on a date
which I do not recall—possibly at the end of March. On
entering the sacristy I found a light was on. I blamed Señora
Auxiliadora Martinez because I believed that she had left it
on. On another date that I do not remember, I again entered
the chapel and found another light turned on—possibly
around the first few days of April. I then blamed Señora
Socorro Barea. I did not think that these signs were coming
from Heaven, and for that reason I would quarrel with these
ladies, because of the cost of electricity. I wanted to tell
them to be more careful with the lights because we have
very little money. The keys had been given to me . . . and
always the one in charge of the keys of a house also is the
one who needs to be the most careful. And that was my
concern.

But when I tried to go and scold them and went to their
home to do so . . . I could not say anything. I saw them as
being innocent—inwardly I could see that—I saw that I was
blaming them without them being at fault. I then thought I
would say nothing, and if anything over the minimum was
spent, I would pay it myself.

On April 15, 1980, I saw the statue all illuminated. I
thought it was the boys playing in the plaza who had broken the roof tiles and that was how the light entered over
the statue. I also thought I would be charging them for the
roof tiles and cost of repair, because I had charged them
once before for this; since then I had not again done so. But
my thought was that they had entered intrusively because I

live far away, and I thought, "Now that I was not there, they played and broke the tiles." I got closer to see, and saw that there was not one hole in the roof; I went over to see if it was through the windows that outside light was coming in and could see nothing. I returned close to the statue to see if someone had placed on her a phosphorescent rosary. I saw the hands, the feet, the neck . . . it was nothing like that. The light was not coming out of anything, the light came from her. That was a great mystery for me; with the light that came from her one could walk without tripping. And it was nighttime, almost eight o'clock at night, as I had arrived late. I then understood that it was a strange thing . . . and that it no longer was an ordinary thing, well . . . for me . . . I thought, "The Holy Virgin, the Holy Mother, is angry with me because I have been quarreling with the people." I decided to ask their forgiveness because I was so moved at seeing her so illuminated . . . I saw her beautiful . . . .

I went to ring the church bell because I arrived an hour late, and with the incident of the illumination it had become even later for the praying of the Rosary. All that I had seen was engraved on my mind, and I thought: "I am the one who is to blame."

As these thoughts were going through my mind, I remembered something that my grandmother used to tell me when I was a child: "Never be a lamp in the street and a darkness at home." I understood my sin: I wanted others to make peace, but I was quarreling in my own house. I say this because I had helped to solve a problem in the town of Cuapa. There was division among the people because many opposed the arrival of Cubans for the literacy program. The chief opponents were the young men who were to teach. They said we could do it all ourselves: professors, students from the scholastic center, and individual volunteers from town. The young men were so violent about it that they said, "If the Father wants Cubans to come here, it is better that he go back to Italy." But, little by little, by talking with the priest, we settled everything without violence. I say that we settled it because no Cubans ever arrived in Cuapa for the literacy program.

But in Comarca del Silencio [a small village on the other side of the mountains, about 10 kilometers east of Cuapa] there was a problem with a young man who became ill, and they had to bring a Cuban in to replace him. It turned out that the Cuban, at seeing that the peasants gave thanks to God for their food, would tell them, "Don't say that...say as we say, 'Thanks to Fidel that I have eaten.'" This proved that we had good reason for not wanting to have Cubans in Cuapa because this young man had been taught to put man in the place of God.

I thought about all this and returned to the thought that I was able to help bring peace there, but in my own house I was not doing this. [It is interesting to note, especially in light of Bernardo's ordination in August 1995 as a priest of the Catholic Church, that Bernardo considers "the Church" his home.] And in this way I decided to ask for their forgiveness in front of all the people. I did that. They forgave me.

After the public apology, I told all the people, who were there praying the Rosary, what I had seen: the illuminated statue. But I asked them to keep it secret. It was not so. The secret spread throughout all of Cuapa, and I suffered due to this because some of them ridiculed me.

One of the sisters in the community went to Juigalpa and told it to the priest who also is our rector. Whenever he arrived at Cuapa he would say to me, "What news do you have?" I would say there was no news and he would insist, "You do have something."

One day I arrived at the house of Señora Consuelo Marin, and she asked me. I told her everything that had occurred, and she in turn told me that she believed it and to tell the Virgin that she wanted to see her illuminated. She made me promise that I would let her know if I again saw her.

The priest, our pastor, on another day again asked me and related to me all that had been told to him. I told him yes, that it was true. He told me to tell it all again to him. I related it to him. He asked me what it was that I prayed. I told him the Rosary and three Hail Marys to the Holy Virgin ever since I was little. And that my grandmother had taught me to call upon her always when I had any tribulations, saying, "Don't leave me, my Mother." She also taught me to say:

It is Mary our Helper, sweet lighthouse of the sea.
Since I first learned to love, the love of my soul is she.
Each of my childhood steps she did guide,
And for that, since childhood, my love for her abides.

She taught me this from memory because she did not know how to read. The pastor then told me to pray and to ask the Blessed Virgin if there was anything that she wanted from us, and to more clearly manifest herself. I did so, but I prayed like this:

> Blessed Mother, please do not request anything of me. I have many problems in the Church. Make your request known to some other person because I want to avoid any more problems. I have a great many now. I don't want any more.

That is what I would say to the Holy Virgin.

As the days passed, the people began to forget about the illumination of the statue. I, for my part, continued with my prayer as the priest ordered.

Now I understand that is how the Holy Virgin wanted to prepare me, the same as a farmer would prepare the soil. With that public confession I made before my brothers...with which I asked for forgiveness . . . I was the place wherein a change took place. I was changed; by this she prepared me.

The May Apparitions

Early in May I felt sad because of financial problems, employment problems, and even spiritual problems. And I felt bored. I had even said in the morning that I wished to die. I didn't want to exist. I had worked a great deal for the people of the town, and I could see that they did not appreciate anything. I had no desire to keep going. In the chapel I swept . . . I removed the dust . . . I washed the altar cloths and albs . . . and for this very same thing I was scorned, I was called a fool. Even my own family—my blood brother— would say that I did not prosper financially because of my involvement with things at the sacristy. I have been a sacristan but without earning any money for this. I began to work

in the house of God since I was able to use the dust cloth and
the broom . . . . I was at the time very small. I have done it
because in that way I serve the Lord. At any rate, now in
Cuapa everything has changed, because sweeping the chapel
is an honor. It is now an honor! The altar cloths are washed in
the blink of an eye, before you are able to notice they are
washed and ironed.

Returning to how I was feeling in the early days of May, I
hardly slept on the night of the seventh. All night I felt very
hot and feeling this heat I got up. I ate something and said to
myself, "I will go to the river to fish so that I will feel cool and
more tranquil." I left early in the morning with a sack and a
machete. I went to the river . . . and I felt happy . . . con-
tented...in a pleasant environment. And I forgot all my problems. When it was twelve noon I did not want to leave
because I felt tranquility . . . joy . . . . And I felt no hunger. At
one o'clock, it rained and I went to the base of a tree; I started
to pray the Rosary. As the rain was stopping I was finishing
the Rosary. I was all wet, my clothes all soaked. I collected the
fish which were in the sand, put them in a sack, and went to a
mango tree to see if the fruit were ripe. I then went to a hill to
cut a branch to gather coyoles [a small round fruit that grows in
Nicaragua]. Immediately after, I went to a jocote tree to pick
jocotes [another Nicaraguan fruit]. I then thought it must be late. I
looked at the sun because I do not have a watch. For us in the
country, the sun is our clock where we read the time. It was
three o'clock in the afternoon. The hours had been like minutes. I said to myself, "It is late." I remembered that I had to
feed the animals and then go to town to pray the Rosary with
the people at five.

I left then, walking from the jocotes in the direction of the
coyoles trees, when suddenly I saw a lightning flash. I
thought and said to myself, "It is going to rain." But I became
filled with wonder because I did not see from where the lightning had come. I stopped but I could see nothing—no signs of
rain. Afterward, I went over near a place where there are
some rocks. I walked about six or seven steps. That was when
I saw another lightning flash, but that was to open my vision,
and she presented herself.

I was then wondering whether this could be something bad, whether it was the same statue as in the chapel. But I saw that she blinked and that she was beautiful. She remained above the pile of rocks as if on a cloud. And there was a little tree on top of the rocks and over that tree was the cloud. The cloud was extremely white. It radiated in all directions the rays of the sun light. On the cloud were the feet of a very beautiful lady. Here feet were bare. The dress was long and white with a celestial cord around the waist, and it had long sleeves. Covering her was a veil, a pale cream color, with gold embroidery along the edge. Her hands were held together over her breast. It looked like the statue of the Virgin of Fatima. I was immobile. I had no inclination to run, to yell. I felt no fear. I was surprised. I thought and said, "What am I seeing? Could it be the same statue of the Virgin from the chapel in Cuapa that they brought and placed here? Is it an attempt to play a joke on me because I said I saw it illuminated? Is this a trick? But no! I would have seen them carrying it." I then passed my hand over my face because I thought that what I saw was a dream. And I said, "Could it be that I am asleep, but I have not tripped over anything?"

And when I removed my hands from my face I saw that she had human skin and that her eyes moved and blinked. I then said, in my thoughts because I could not move my tongue—I said, "She is alive . . . she is not a statue! She is alive!" My mind was the only thing that I could move. I felt like numb, my lower jaw stiff and my tongue as if asleep; everything immobilized, as I said, only the ideas moved in my head. I was in those thoughts when she extended her arms—like the Miraculous Medal which I never had seen but which later was shown to me. She extended her arms and from her hands emanated rays of light stronger than the sun and the rays that came from her hands touched my breast. [Bernardo's description, which he conveyed to Chilean artist Raimundo Rubio, was the inspiration for Rubio's painting of "Our Lady of Nicaragua" that adorns the cover of this book.]

When she gave out her light is when I became encouraged to speak, although somewhat stammering, I said to her, "What is your name?" She answered me with the sweetest voice I have ever heard in any woman, not even in persons who speak softly. She answered me and said that her name is Mary. I saw the way she moved her lips. I then said, "She is alive! She spoke! She has answered my question!" I could see that we could enter into a conversation, that I could speak with her. I asked her, then, where she came from.

She told me with the same sweetness, *"I come from Heaven. I am the Mother of Jesus."*

At hearing this, I immediately—remembering what the priest had told me—asked her, "What is it you want?"

She answered me, *"I want the Rosary to be prayed every day."*

I then interrupted and said to her, "Yes, we are praying it . . . . The priest brought us the intentions of the San Francisco parish so that we would unite ourselves with them."

She told me:

I don't want it prayed only in the month of May. I want it to be prayed permanently, within the family . . . including the children old enough to understand . . . to be prayed at a set hour when there are no problems with the work in the home.

She told me that the Lord does not like prayers we make in a rush or mechanically. Because of that she recommended praying of the Rosary accompanied with the reading of biblical citations and that we put into practice the Word of God. When I heard this I thought and said, "How is this?" Because I did not know the Rosary was biblical. That is why I asked her and said, "Where are the biblical citations?" She told me to look for them in the Bible and continued saying:

Love each other.
Fulfill your obligations.
Make peace. Don't ask Our Lord for peace because, if you do not make it, there will be no peace.

Afterward, she told me:

Renew the five first Saturdays. You received many graces when all of you did this.

Before the war we used to do this—we went to Confession and Communion every first Saturday of the month—but since the Lord already had freed us from the shedding of blood in Cuapa, we no longer continued this practice.

Then she said:

Nicaragua has suffered much since the earthquake. She is threatened with even more suffering. She will continue to suffer if you don't change.

[A massive earthquake hit Nicaragua shortly before Christmas in December 1972 practically destroying all of downtown Managua, the capitol of Nicaragua. Over 10,000 people are believed to have been killed.]

And after a brief pause she said:

Pray, pray, my son, the Rosary for all the world. Tell believers and non-believers that the world is threatened by grave dangers. I ask the Lord to appease His justice, but, if you don't change, you will hasten the arrival of a Third World War.

After she had said these words, I understood that I had to tell this to the people, and I told her, "Lady, I don't want problems. I have many in the Church. Tell this to another person."

She then told me: *"No, because Our Lord has selected you to give the message."*

When she told me this, I saw that the cloud which was holding her was rising, and I recalled what Señora Consuelo Marin had said, and I told her, "Lady, don't go because I want to go and notify Señora Consuelo because she told me that she wanted to see you.

She said to me, *"No. Not everyone can see me. She will see me when I take her to Heaven, but she should pray the Rosary as I ask."*

And after telling me this the cloud continued to rise. She raised her arms to Heaven as in the statue of the Assumption, which I have seen so many times in the Cathedral at Juigalpa.

She again looked upward toward Heaven, and the cloud that held her slowly elevated her as if she was in a ray of light. When she reached a certain height she disappeared.

I then gathered the machete, the sack, and the branch. I went to cut the coyoles, and thought I would tell no one— to say nothing of what I had seen or heard.

I went to the chapel to pray the Rosary and did not mention what had happened. When I returned home I felt sad. My problems increased with that. I prayed the Rosary again, and I asked the Blessed Mother to free me from temptations because I thought that is what it was—a temptation. During the night I heard a voice saying to me that I should tell. I awoke again, and I again prayed the Rosary. I could not find peace. I did not tell anyone because I did not want the people to talk. They were already talking because I had seen the statue illuminated. I thought, "Now it will be worse. I will never have peace." That is why it was that I did not want to say anything. And I did not return to the place of the apparitions. The mangoes and jocotes were lost to me. I went to the river, but by another road. I go to the river every day to bathe and to give water to the calf that I have.

During this period that I was guarding the secret, a great weight seemed to fall on me, and I heard something like a voice which told me to tell. But I simply did not want to tell, since the suffering was greater each time. I sought ways to distract myself. I sought out my friends in order to be entertained—young friends and old friends—but always at the height of the merriment I heard the voice and the sadness would return. I was getting thin and pale. People asked what was wrong, if I was sick. I told them "No." Eight days like that passed.

On the 16th of May I was enroute to give water to the calf. I was crossing the pasture unable to see the calf. I was walking with a stick in my hand. As I was near a tree, already halfway through the pasture, with the strong sun directly overhead, I saw a lightning flash. It was twelve noon. In plain light, because, as I said, it was a hot sunny day, there was another even stronger light—more light then the midday light. In that lightning flash she presented herself. I saw her in the same way as I had seen her on the 8th of May, with her hands together, and then she extended them. And on extending her hands, the rays of light came toward me. I remained watching her. I remained silent, but I said to myself, "It is she! She is the same one. The same lady has again appeared to me." I thought she had come to complain about all that she had told me to say. I felt guilty for not having spoken as she had asked, and at the same time, in my mind, I said, "I don't go to the place where she appeared because she appears there, and now, she appears to me here. I will be in a fine state, she will be following me wherever I am."

It was with this in mind, when she told me with her voice soft, but with a tone as of in reprehension, *"Why have you not told what I sent you to tell?"*

I then answered her, "Lady, it is that I am afraid. I am afraid of being the ridicule of the people, afraid that they will laugh at me, that they will not believe me. Those who will not believe this will laugh at me. They will say that I am crazy."

She then said to me, *"Do not be afraid. I am going to help you, and go tell the priest."* Saying this, there was another flash of lightning and she disappeared. I then continued walking and saw the calf I was unable to see before. I took it to the river, gave it some water, and returned to my house. I got ready to go to the chapel, and then I prayed the Rosary.

I thought of telling it only to Señora Lillian Ruiz de Martinez and to Señora Socorro Barea de Marin. That is what I did. I have more trust in them than in any other person in the community of Cuapa. I called them aside and told them all that I had seen and heard. They then reprimanded me. It was the first time I received correction without answering back, because I always attempted to come out with my own ideas. And I would grumble. I promised them that I would tell it the next day. I went home and lay down to sleep. The next day dawned and I felt a strange happiness. All the problems, it seemed to me, had dissipated. It was the 17th of May.

On that day I told everyone who came to my house. I told them and they heard me. Some of them believed, others listened out of curiosity and pretended, others did not believe and laughed. But that did not matter to me at all. When it was time to pray the Rosary, we prayed it, and afterward I told them everything. Again I noticed the same thing: Some believed, others did not, some remained listening in wonder . . . amazed . . . others as if analyzing, others remained silent, others laughed and said I was crazy—each one according to how he felt. But none of it was important to me. I felt happiness at saying everything.

On the 19th of May I went to Juigalpa in the morning, and I told the priest as the Lady had told me. He asked, "Would it be someone who wants to frighten you in those hills?"

I told him, "No." I said, "No," because there was a possibility to do this at the river or in the hills where I had gone to cut the stick, but not in the middle of the pasture where I was walking; there was no way. Nothing can be hidden. It is open field.

He then said to me, "Could it be a temptation that persecutes you?"

I told him, "No" . . . . I did not know that because I could only relate to him what I had seen and heard. But regarding the temptation, I could not say because I did not know.

He then told me to go to the place where the apparitions occurred and to pray the Rosary there, to make the Sign of the Cross when I saw her and do not be afraid, because whether it was something evil or good, nothing was going to happen to me. He also told me not to tell anyone what I saw or heard, afterward. But what I had already seen, I could tell the people of Cuapa.

This apparition I take as a continuation of the one on the 8th of May, and I call it the one of The Reclamation.

The June Dreams with
the Blessed Virgin Mary

On the 8th of June I went to the site where the apparitions took place because she had asked me to be there. I arrived and prayed the Rosary with some persons, but Our Lady did not arrive. I returned feeling disconsolate.

During the night, in dreams, she presented herself. It was the same as during the day—I was at the same place where I saw her the first time. I prayed the Rosary. Upon finishing the Rosary, I again saw the two lightning flashes and she appeared. In my dream, She gave me the same message as she had done the first time, and afterward I told her some

requests which I had, because by now the people would recommend to me things to tell her. She answered me by saying,
"Some will be fulfilled, others will not."

And I remained without knowing which ones would be
fulfilled and which would not. The petitions that the people of Cuapa made to me were varied: some such as, "to
have good luck with work," "that I will earn more money,"
"that I will be cured of some illness," and other problems.
Others requested something spiritual, such as, "to have
patience," "love for God," "faith," "perseverance in prayer,"
"to be able to love the ones who do not like me and who are
harmful to my loved ones." As it turned out, I was unable
to tell the people which would be granted and which
would not.

Our Lady presented herself over the little Morisco tree as
she did the first time. She faced the east. To her left, near the
pile of rocks where the little tree grew, were two cedars. At
present one no longer exists because the people have been
taking the trunk bit by bit; the other one also is disappearing.
So the cedars are no longer cedars; stripped, without foliage
and branches, they are dry. The only part remaining is the
part where the trunk is attached to the roots. Of the little
Morisco tree nothing remains; it has totally disappeared. To
her right but a little farther away, there are four coyole palms.
Between the first and the second, as one comes from the river
there is a large open space. Raising her right hand, she
pointed toward that space and said, *"Look at the sky."*

I looked at that direction. A tree that is in front, between
the two palms, did not impede my ability to see because it
has few branches and it is low. She presented something like
a movie in that space I mentioned. I saw a large group of people who were dressed in white and were walking toward
where the sun rises. They were bathed in light and very
happy; they sang. I could hear them, but I could not understand the words. It was a celestial festival. It was such happiness . . . such joy . . . which I had never ever seen. Not even in
a procession had I seen that. Their bodies radiated light. I felt
as if I were transported. Nor can I myself explain it . . . in the
midst of my admiration I heard her tell me:

Look. These are the very first communities when Christianity began. They are the first catechumens; many of them were martyrs. Do you people want to be martyrs? Would you yourself like to be a martyr?

In that instance I did not know exactly what the meaning of being a martyr was—I now know, because I have been asking, that it is he who professes Jesus Christ openly in public, he who is a witness to Him including the giving of his life—but, I answered, "Yes."

After that I saw another group, also dressed in white with some luminous rosaries in their hands. The beads were extremely white and they gave off lights of different colors. One of them carried a very large open book. He would read, and after listening they silently meditated. They appeared to be as if in prayer. After this period of prayer in silence, they then prayed the Our Father and ten Hail Marys. I prayed with them. When the Rosary was finished, Our Lady said to me:

These are the first ones to whom I gave the Rosary. That is the way I want all of you to pray the Rosary.

I answered the Lady that, yes, we would. (Some persons have told me that this possibly has to do with the Dominicans. I do not know that religious order and to this date have never seen anyone from that order.)

Afterward, I saw a third group, all of them dressed in brown robes. But these I recognized as being similar to the Franciscans. Always the same, with rosaries and praying. As they were passing after having prayed, Our Lady again told me:

These received the Rosary from the hands of the first ones.

After this, a fourth group was arriving. It was a huge procession. This group was dressed as we dress. It was such a big group that it would be impossible to count them. In the earlier ones I saw many men and women; but now, it was like an army in size, and they carried rosaries in their hands. They were dressed normally, in all colors. I was very happy to see them. When one is dressed differently from other persons one feels rather strange . . . at seeing the first group I did not feel so attracted to them because of that . . . I admired them, but I did not feel as if in their midst as when I saw the last group. I felt at once that I could enter into that scene because they were dressed the same as I was. But . . . I looked at my hands and saw them black. They, in turn, as the previous ones, radiated light. Their bodies were beautiful. I then said, "Lady, I am going with these because they are dressed as I am."

She told me, *"No. You are still lacking. You have to tell the people what you have seen and heard."* And she added:

> *I have shown you the Glory of Our Lord, and you people will acquire this if you are obedient to Our Lord, to the Lord's Word; if you persevere in praying the Holy Rosary and put into practice the Lord's Word.*

After having said this to me the Vision of the Glory of God disappeared, and the cloud that was sustaining her elevated her toward Heaven. She looked like, as I said, the statue of the Assumption. And in that way, with the cloud lifting her, she disappeared.

I was under a prohibition from the priest from telling what I saw and heard. I could tell it only to him. I took the bus early on the morning on the 9th of June, and I told it to the priest. I thought that once I had told him, he then would right away give me permission to tell it. It was not so. When I realized that he was not telling me, "Tell the people," I then asked him for permission and he said, "No"—for me to keep it in secret. I then began to feel a tremendous weight and sorrow which I could hardly stand, and I kept hearing a voice telling me to tell it. I began suffering as I had before. But I chose to obey the priest, and I did not relate it until permission was given.

Permission was finally given to me on the 24th of June, which is the patron feast of Cuapa [the feast day of the Birth of St. John the Baptist] to tell it but only to the people in that village. On that day the church was full of people, and I went to wait to meet with the priest to ask permission. The priest told me, "No," twice, and the third time accepted that I tell it.

The July Dream with the Angel

On the 8th of July about 40 of us went to the place where the apparitions occurred. We prayed and sang, but I did not see her. I begged in my prayers that I would see her again. At night, while sleeping, I had a dream. I dreamed that I was in the place of the apparitions praying for the world. In my dream I remembered that Our Lady had told me to pray for Nicaragua and for the whole world because serious dangers threaten it. I then, remembering this and that the priest had told me—when I had told him the message from the Holy Virgin—to pray especially for the religious, the nuns, the priests, and the Pope—remembering all of that, I started praying; I began commending them. And I commended the whole world in the Rosary.

Now there was a boy from Cuapa who was in jail. There had been a fight at a fiesta; they had accused him of being a counterrevolutionary and took him prisoner after the war. His sister asked me to make a petition for him. She was very sad because she could not speak with him alone when she visited him in jail. And, furthermore, they would not leave them alone to talk. So, after I finished the Rosary, I realized that I had not prayed for this boy, and I thought, "I am going to pray for him, but the Rosary is taking me a long time . . . ." (I was thinking this in my dreams since I believed myself to be at the place of the apparitions.) I said to myself, "I have to get home; it will be getting too late when I return . . . I am only going to pray three Hail Marys."

In my dream, I knelt down and raised up my arms. I again looked upward praying for the boy. When I lowered my eyes and looked at the rocks where the Holy Virgin has appeared, I saw an angel. He was dressed in a long white tunic. He was tall and very young. His body appeared to be bathed in light. He had a man's physique and voice. He carried no adornment, no mantle, nor a crown. Plain but beautiful. His feet were not over a cloud. They were bare. He had a warm, friendly demeanor and a great serenity. I felt a reverence as I was before him, but my feeling toward him was different from what I felt before the Lady . . . as if she were someone greater . . . she greater than he . . . I don't know how to explain it, it is difficult to say. . . . Nonetheless, in spite of the fact that she inspired within me more respect, that is . . . like a great respect, a greater reverence, than that which I felt toward the angel, with her I was bold enough to ask questions, and I spoke to her and made petitions. With the angel I hardly spoke. I heard the angel tell me, *"Your prayer has been heard."*

After a moment of silence he added:

> *Go and tell the prisoner's sister to go and console him on Sunday as he is very sad; to advise him not to sign a document; that they are going to pressure him to sign a paper in which he assumes responsibility for some money; he is innocent.*
>
> *That she should not worry that she will be able to talk to him alone for a long time; that she will be treated in a friendly manner.*
>
> *To go on Monday to the police headquarters of Juigalpa to complete all the steps for his release because he will be released that day.*
>
> *To take 1,000 córdobas because they are charging a fine.*

I then told him that I had another petition from a cousin who lives in Zelaya [another Department into which Nicaragua is divided, east of Chontales]. She had come to Cuapa to see me and to ask me to speak to the Holy Virgin about two problems: problems in the home as a result of the vice of drink and problems with work due to the changes brought about by the revolution. She wanted to know how to resolve the vice of alcoholism with her father and brother, because the resulting problems at home were caused by their violence when they drink too much. She also wanted to know what she could do with her problems at work as a teacher. She explained to me that she did not want to lose her job, but it seemed as if little by little they would cause her to deny her faith. In this she was suffering a great deal because she did not want to lose her work, but even less so to deny her faith.

That is why I told the angel that I had two petitions for the Blessed Virgin from a cousin, and without entering into details, I told him that it was with regard to problems in the home because of the father's and brother's vice with drinking, and also problems with work. I did not go into any more details. The angel answered me saying, *"The persons around them should be patient with them, and not to complain when they are inebriated."* Later he added, *"Go and tell them to discontinue with that vice, to do it little by little, and in that way the desire will leave them."*

He then told me to warn my (other) cousin that they were going to assault him; they were going to shoot him in the foot wounding his left heel. And at a later time they were going to kill him. On hearing this, I became so frightened that I told the angel, "Won't that sentence upon my cousin be revoked by praying many Rosaries?" He answered, *"No. It is from that he will die, but, if he listens to your advice, his life can be prolonged."* He then added for my other cousin, *"That she should not be afraid. To stay firmly where she is. That she should not leave her job because as a teacher who has faith in Our Lord she can do a lot of good with people."* And he continued, saying, *"Do not turn your back on problems and do not curse anyone."*

This, the angel told me at the end and disappeared. I awoke. I immediately began to pray the Rosary, without being distracted by what I had dreamed. Afterward, I started thinking about all that I had dreamed. I remembered everything as if it had remained impressed on me. I did not know what to think. But I chose to tell it to the prisoner's sister in secret because I feared it might not be fulfilled. The people were commenting over the Glory of God that I had seen on the 8th of June and they said, "Who has gone there (Heaven) and who has returned? Bernardo is crazy. We should take him to the asylum." That is why I was afraid. I told it to Señora Socorro telling her it was only for her alone. I told it to her the next day. She asked me how this could be as she was not allowed to speak with him alone. I told her to have confidence in the Lord and to go and do everything the angel said. Together we prayed the Rosary for the brother who was in jail.

She went to see him on Sunday, the 13th of July. She was in the jail a long time with him alone, and because of that she was able to tell him not to sign the document. They were all friendly with her. When she returned to Cuapa, the same day, Sunday, in the afternoon, she asked for a loan of 1,000 córdobas from a man who never lends anything without impounding something. He gave it to her without any warranties, without a bond, and even said to her, "If you want more, I will give you more."

They presented the document to the boy, but he refused to sign it. Señora Socorro went on Monday to the police headquarters in Juigalpa to complete all the necessary steps to see if they would release him. She found the people at the headquarters quite friendly. They freed the brother and charged a fine of 1,000 córdobas. She told them she was poor and could they lower it some, and they reduced it by 200 córdobas. Everything was fulfilled. They soon left and returned to Cuapa and arrived at my house to express their thanks. I told them not to thank me, but to thank the Lord and the Holy Virgin. I suggested to them that they pray the Rosary. Señora Socorro was very happy and asked me if she could tell it to the people. I told her, "Yes." Many came to believe because of this event, which for me and for others was proof of what I had been relating.

He was released from jail on Monday, July 14. The next day I went to Zelaya to tell them of the message received. I spoke to the three of them. She believed me and told me that she could continue working as a teacher. My uncle listened and promised me that he would try to give up the vice little by little. Afterward, I went by horse all the way over to my cousin's ranch, but he did not believe me. He did not believe anything. He listened but out of respect. He was indifferent with me and even hard, because in a tone of voice that was insulting he told me, "Cousin, are you looking for some way to take a drink?"

I returned to my house feeling sad and praying the Rosary for him. A few days later I heard that he had been robbed and his home assaulted. I then returned to Zelaya to give him advice and to tell him to sell his ranch and return to Cuapa. In that way he would avoid those incidents. He paid no attention to me, in spite of the fact that what I had told him in the previous visit was already in part fulfilled: I told him about a robbery. They stole two mules from him. I told him of an assault. They broke in his door one night and again robbed him.

I told him that his left heel would be wounded. And it was so. During this second visit to Zelaya, he showed me the wound himself, but he did not believe. He said it was just by chance. There was no change in him.

I returned to Cuapa feeling sad. Disconsolate! I would pray the Rosary for him.

Two months and one day later, that is, on the 9th of September 1980, his sister-in-law, who lives in Cuapa and who did not believe anything that I said, received a telegram notifying her that my cousin had been found murdered. At twelve midnight of that same day, which was also the day following the third apparition, his body arrived in Cuapa.

I had an appointment with the Lady, but it did not take place. We could not get there because the river was too deep, it was full. The current was too strong, and it was overflowing its banks because of the violent winds. Very heavy rains since the night of the seventh of August, all that night and all the following day . . . it rained without stopping on the day of the 8th of August. It was impossible to cross! I was there accompanied by a group of people, all of them women. On arriving at the edge of the river we intended to cross, we found this impossible. It would have been impossible even on horseback. I said, "Even by myself alone, I am going to cross."

But I looked and said, "No! I can't do it alone! The current will carry me away. It is so strong!" It continued raining. We were totally soaked from the rain. I then told the people, "The Blessed Virgin, the Blessed Mother, will hear us wherever we are." And we stopped trying to cross the river in order to get to the site of the apparitions. We sat down on the rocks alongside the river; others remained standing. We then prayed the Rosary and sang many songs. On our return we did not feel cold, nor were we sad.

When it became possible to cross the river, we returned to the place of the apparitions. But nothing occurred, nor did I feel that the Lady would arrive. I missed not seeing her. I had by now become familiar with the idea of her arriving. I felt happy to be waiting for her and even more so at seeing her.

Another thing that happened during this month is that I could see that the priest did not believe me. Because of good manners he tried not to show this, but . . . no, he did not believe. He had never shown any interest in going to the place where the apparitions occurred. However, one day he arrived at the chapel, celebrated Mass, and afterward told me that he wanted to go to the site where the apparitions took place. But he told me not to point out the road and also not to speak with him.

It was so. We arrived at the place. I could see that he looked at all the sides around us. He looked as if recognizing something. Afterward, indicating the precise spot, he said, "It is this place that was in my dreams last night."

With this he changed. Prior to this I noted that he did not accept. I could notice it. But I do not judge him, as perhaps he has been an instrument to know the truth.

Toward the end of August, one day I told him, "Father, I am sad because we were unable to cross the river because of the strong currents. Could it be that she expected us to cross the river on the 8th of August? Could it be that she won't be returning?"

He said to me, "Pray, and she will again appear." He said that with certainty.

The September Apparition of the Virgin Mary Appearing as a Child

On the 8th of September I went to the place of the apparitions in hope of the appointment which had not been fulfilled for me in August. I again went accompanied by many people; there were also some children. We were praying the Rosary, and as soon as we finished I saw a lightning flash. Only the light from it was seen. It was three in the afternoon. The day was clear; there was no sign of rain. I thought and said, "The Lady is about to arrive!" Another sign was the great interior joy when I am about to see her. I then saw a second flash of lightning—which is always the one in which to see her—and I saw her over a cloud.

The cloud was over the Morisco tree that was already without leaves—the people of Cuapa had been taking them little by little—the little tree, planted in the midst of the rocks and of the Dormilona thorns looked dried up; because the Morisco tree is brown in color and having been left without leaves, it looked more as if it was dried up. But no, it was not dry; if one scratched the bark which is thin, it was green inside. In this manner, over all of this, was the Virgin Mary.

I saw her as a child. Beautiful! But little! She was dressed in a pale cream colored tunic. She did not have a veil, nor a crown, nor a mantle. No adornment, nor embroidery. The dress was long, with long sleeves, and it was girdled with a pink cord. Her hair fell to her shoulders and it was brown in color. The eyes, also, although much lighter, almost the color of honey. All of her radiated light. She looked like the Lady, but she was a child.

I was looking at her amazed without saying a word, and then I heard her voice as that of a child . . . a child of seven . . . eight . . . years. In an extremely sweet voice she gave me a message—totally identical. At the finish, I thought that since she was a child it would be easier for her to allow herself to be seen by the others accompanying me. That was my goal. I said to myself, "The others should also see her!" I then told her, "Let yourself be seen so that all the world will believe. These people who are here want to meet you." The people could hear me, but could not hear her. I talked with her a great deal trying to entice her to allow herself to be seen, but after listening to me she said:

No. It is enough for you to give them the message because for the one who is going to believe that will be enough, and the one who is not going to believe though he should see me is not going to believe.

These words of hers have been fulfilled. I can now see the unbelief or the faith of a person: Individuals have come who are not looking to see any sign; the message is sufficient for them, they receive it. Some have great needs . . . they do not ask for a miracle, they do not ask for cures; they prefer to trust in the Lord. There are others who through the signs have come to believe. I knew a man, who filled with joy, told me, "Bernardo, I now do believe the Virgin appeared. You are fortunate! I also am seeing her!" And he indicated the place. It was in the old chapel, where the altar was before.

A few feet away there was another man who, at seeing me pass nearby, told me full of indifference, "It is true that it is here. But this is nothing more than beings from other planets. They are UFOs." This occurred on the 7th of May 1981, the eve of the first anniversary of the first apparition.

I no longer insisted that she allow herself to be seen, but rather I talked to her about the church that the people wanted to build in her honor. Father Domingo told us that this was a decision he could not make, and that we should tell it to the Holy Virgin. That is why I presented this question to her. Because a man from Matagalpa had already given me 80 córdobas to this end. She answered me, saying:

No. The Lord does not want material churches. He wants living temples which are yourselves. Restore the sacred temple of the Lord. In you is the gratification for the Lord.

And she continued, saying:

Love each other. Love One another.
Forgive each other.
Make peace. Don't just ask for it. Make peace!

I asked what I should do with the 80 córdobas that I had on my hands. I was wondering if I should return them. She told me to donate them for the construction of the chapel in Cuapa, and added:

From this day on do not accept even one cent for anything.

[Bernardo subsequently explained that the Virgin knew that the Sandinistas were going to offer him four farms to profane the message. As she knew this, she wanted him to accept nothing.] Afterward, she told me not to say "church" in reference to material things because we, ourselves, were the church and the temples; those (material buildings) were chapels or houses of prayer. At times, out of habit I make a mistake and say "church" instead of "chapel." At this moment, a doubt that I had previously had came to mind. I had thought of asking her as to this doubt because I did not know whether or not to continue in the catechumenate [the preparation of adults for receiving baptism and the other sacraments of initiation in the Catholic Church]. I did it to see what she would advise me. She told me:

> *No. Don't leave. Always continue firmly in the catechumenate. Little by little you will comprehend all that the catechumenate signifies. As a community group, meditate on the Beautitudes, away from all the noise.*

Later she added:

> *I am not going to return on the 8th of October, but on the 13th.*

Then the cloud elevated her, as in the other times when I had seen her.

The October Apparition

In October, on the 8th, we went to the site of the apparitions. I knew she would not appear because the little girl already had told me that, and I told the people. People by now were following me, but they wanted to pray the Rosary near the pile of rocks. They wanted to do this out of devotion.

On the 13th, which was a Monday, we had a celebration in the chapel at ten in the morning. Afterward a group of about fifty of us went to the site of the apparitions. A small pilgrimage. [The pilgrimage would have walked in a westerly direction passing near Bernardo's house and then headed south to the site of the first apparition. Since Bernardo's house was about two kilometers from the chapel and about one kilometer from the apparition site, the pilgrimage was somewhat over three kilometers, which would be approximately two miles.] We went praying the Rosary and singing. On arriving we arranged the flowers the people had brought, over the pile of rocks. We started another Rosary. The sky looked as if it was going to rain, with big threatening clouds. It looked like rain. When we were on the third mystery, the birth of the Son of God, I felt the same emotion that I always feel when the moment for seeing her is near. But I chose not to disturb the praying of the Rosary.

When we finished the Rosary, we sang "Holy Queen of Heaven." We were repeating the part that says, "Shining Day Star, grant me grace to be able to sing the Ave Maria," when all of a sudden a big luminous circle formed over the ground. Everyone, without a single exception, saw it. It was like a single ray that fell and marked this luminous circle on the ground. The light came from above. The light that came was like a spotlight that, on touching the ground, was scattered. Seeing how this light fell over the heads of everyone who was there, I again looked upward and saw that a circle had also formed in the sky, as when we say, "There's a ring around the moon," or, "There's a ring around the sun." This circle gave off lights in different colors, without coming from the sun. It was not at that spot as the sun was already setting.

A little girl being held by the hand by her mother tried to release her hand telling her mother that the Lady was calling her. The mother held her even more firmly and did not let her move. (The child's mother told me this herself after the apparition was over.)

It was three in the afternoon. One could feel a small breeze that moved softly. Pleasant! Like a fresh shower, but which did not wet us. While we observed this, we were silent and continued seeing that circle of light which gave off colored lights from the exact center, where the sun is at twelve noon.

All of a sudden a lightning flash, the same as the other times; then, a second one. I lowered my eyes and I saw the Lady. This time the cloud was over the flowers we had brought and upon the cloud the Lady's feet. Beautiful! She extended her hands and rays of light reached all of us.

I, at seeing the Lady there with her arms extended, said to the people, "Look at her! There she is!"

No one answered anything. I then told the Lady to let herself be seen, that all the people present wanted to see her. She said, *"No. Not everyone can see me."*

I again said to the people, "Our Lady is at the pile of rocks over the flowers."

I could hear some of the people crying. I could hear something. A lady whose name is Mildred told me, "I can see only a shadow, like a statue, over the flowers." I again insisted to the Lady that she allow herself to be seen, and she again told me, "No."

I then again told the people, "Look at the flowers over the rocks." No one answered me anything. I then told the Lady, "Lady, let them see you so that they will believe! Because many don't believe. They tell me that it is the devil that appears to me, and that the Virgin is dead and turned to dust like any mortal. Let them see you, Our Lady!"

She did not answer anything. She raised her hands to her breast in a similar position to the statue of Our Lady of Sorrows—the statue that is carried in procession during Holy Week—and the same as that statue, her face turned pale, her mantle changed to a gray color, her face became sad, and she cried. I cried too. I trembled to see her like that. I said to her, "Lady, forgive me for what I have said to you! I'm to blame! You are angry with me. Forgive me! Forgive me!"

She then answered me saying: *"I am not angry nor will I get angry."*

I asked her, "And why are you crying?"

She told me:

It saddens me to see the hardness of those persons' hearts. But you will have to pray for them so that they will change.

I could not speak. I continued to cry. I felt that my heart was being crushed. I felt very sad as if I were going to die from the pain right there. My only relief was through crying. I no longer continued insisting that she let herself be seen. I felt that I was to blame for having said this to her. I could not endure seeing her cry. As I continued to cry, she gave the message:

Pray the Rosary, meditate on the mysteries.
Listen to the Word of God spoken in them.
Love one another. Love each other.
Forgive each other.
Make peace. Don't ask for peace without making peace,
     because if you don't make it, it does no good to ask
     for it.
Fulfill your obligations.
Put into practice the Word of God.

Seek ways to please God.
Serve your neighbor, as that way you will please Him.

When she had finished giving her message, I remembered the requests from the people of Cuapa. I said to her, "Lady, I have many requests, but I have forgotten them. There are a great many. You, Lady, know them all."
Then she said to me:

> *They ask of me things that are unimportant.*
> *Ask for faith in order to have the strength so that each can carry his own cross.*
> *The sufferings of this world cannot be removed. Suffering is the cross that all of you have to carry.*
> *That is the way life is. There are problems with the husband, with the wife, with the children, with the brothers. Talk, converse so that problems will be resolved in peace. Do not turn to violence. Never turn to violence.*
> *Pray for faith in order that you will have patience.*

In this manner she has given me to understand that, if with faith we ask to be free from a suffering, we will be free if that suffering is not the cross we are to carry; but when the suffering is that person's cross, then it will remain as a weight of glory. That is why she tells us to ask for faith in order to receive fortitude and patience.
Afterward she told me, *"You will no longer see me in this place."*
I thought that I would definitely never see her again and I began to shout:

Don't leave us, my Mother!
Don't leave us, my Mother!
Don't leave us, my Mother!

I was speaking for those who were not speaking. She then said to me:

> *Do not be grieved. I am with all of you even though you do not see me. I am the Mother of all of you, sinners.*

Love one another. Forgive each other. Make peace, because if you don't make it there will be no peace. Do not turn to violence. Never turn to violence.

Nicaragua has suffered a great deal since the earthquake and will continue to suffer if all of you don't change. If you don't change you will hasten the coming of the Third World War.

Pray, pray, my son, for all the world. Grave dangers threaten the world.

A mother never forgets her children. And I have not forgotten what you suffer. I am the Mother of all of you, sinners. Invoke me with these words: "Holy Virgin, you are my Mother, the Mother to all of us, sinners."

And after having said this three times, she was elevated as if the cloud were pushing her. When she was in the direction of the branches of the cedar, she disappeared.

With this I conclude the report of the apparitions of the Holy Virgin in the Valley of Cuapa in the year 1980.

The important thing is the message. We can accept it or we can reject it. We are free. The Lord respects our freedom.

I am no more than a decayed cane through which the message is passed. In my ignorance, I say it poorly, but the Lord substitutes for this poorness.

We should feel fortunate for this wonder the Lord has done in our midst, and let us be assured that if we so resolve He will be our Peace—the Peace which we have to make in Nicaragua and in the entire world. The Holy Virgin tells us to make Peace and the Peace is Jesus Christ.

I will never cease repeating the message. For as long as my tongue has movement, I will shout it to the four winds.

PART II

The following is the edited text of Bernardo's interview in the Weglian's home in McLean, Virginia, on Monday, January 18, 1993. Most of the questions were framed by Stephen in English, then translated into Spanish and asked by Miriam.

Miriam: It is a great pleasure to have Mr. Bernardo Martinez, of Nicaragua, with us today. He is going to tell us several of the experiences he has had in his country, focusing primarily on the events which occurred after 1980. We would also like to have Bernardo tell us something about his life. Then, we will talk about the history of the statue that illuminated in Cuapa. Finally, we are going to ask him questions on some other subjects of interest that may not have been previously covered. So, welcome, Bernardo! We are very glad to have you here with us today.

Bernardo: Well, it is also a great pleasure for me to be here with you all, sharing the experiences the Blessed Virgin has given me, and to tell you the story of her apparitions. I will certainly be glad to tell you about my life and my childhood. I am very glad to be with you and tell you these things because what these messages contain is very beautiful.

El Crucero Apparition

Miriam: Bernardo, we would like to know whether you saw any apparitions of the Blessed Virgin Mary after 1980.

45

Bernardo: Yes, in 1987 I saw an apparition of the Virgin in Our Lady of Victory Church in El Crucero. [El Crucero is a small town near Managua. It is located at kilometer 24 on the south highway leading from Managua to the border with Costa Rica. Distances are measured from a marker in downtown Managua.] It was like this. When I came to Managua, fleeing from the persecution the Sandinista government had unleashed against me, I hid for four years at the Minor Seminary. Later, in 1986, I asked the Bishop to allow me to work at Our Lady of Victory Church, because the pastor, Msgr. Andino, was very old. The Bishop gave me permission, and I went to help Msgr. Andino. I saw that a lot had to be done, and I didn't even know where to begin.

I asked Msgr. Oswaldo Mondragon to assign some of the students from the Minor Seminary to help me, and he sent me twelve boys. They had just entered the seminary, so they did not have a lot of instruction. I went to the Jesuits' residence where I bought some copies of the Catechism. I began teaching the boys so they, in turn, could teach the people. It was then that the Sandinista government began a great persecution against the young people in order to draft them into military service.

I am not against military service, but these young boys were being taken away without any training whatsoever. They were just being taken to die on Nicaragua's mountain countryside. So, I was afraid the boys that were staying with me would also be taken away. Near the place the boys and I had meetings, there was a house where the militia men were staying. The militia would stare at us as if thinking, "Those boys are so much at peace, and here we are with these rifles . . . ." There is always a revengeful, resentful spirit (i.e., those that want to "get even"), isn't there, in some who find themselves in a harder position than those who are not in the same position? I was afraid of that.

It was on March 7, 1987, that the group of boys and I went to the sacristy of the church to sleep. I locked the doors and put wooden sticks against them so they could not be opened from outside, because it also happened that the soldiers entered the homes at night to take away the boys. They would not do it in the daytime, but at night, like an abduction, and the boys disappeared. Only God knows where they were taken. Their parents would not know, only the authorities. Therefore, I could not go to sleep, because I was concerned for the boys.

The boys were asleep in different rooms, and I would think: "Maybe they (the militia) are going to come to take them away, but here we have some clubs and we are not going to let them do it. It is better to die here—I would think—than to go and die on the mountains." Now, this was humanly speaking, because religiously speaking, you cannot do that. Humanly speaking, because I am a man just like any other man, I thought we should beat them with the clubs. But they were better armed; we only had clubs, and they could shoot us and kill us. I was thinking about this when it dawned on me, "This is a temptation from Satan," the idea of beating and hitting people with the clubs. Then I took out my Rosary, I sat up in bed and began to pray it.

It was well beyond midnight when I said to myself, "I am going to rest for a while in order to calm down. Then I will resume praying until I fall asleep," because sometimes I fall asleep praying the Rosary.

It was then that I heard a voice calling me: *"Bernardo!"* I recognized her voice; it was the same sweetest voice I always describe when telling about the apparitions of the Virgin.

I thought, "The Virgin talked to me! Could it be that someone is trying to imitate her voice in order to lure me into opening the door so they can come in and take the boys away?" But then I thought, "No; nobody can imitate her voice." Because some persons, mainly women, have tried to imitate her voice in order to see if I can recognize it and say, "Yes, that is the voice." But no voice is like hers. Then I convinced myself: "Nobody can imitate her, least of all a man!" So, I replied: "Here I am!"

I had not turned the lights on nor opened the doors (they are wooden doors), when I saw a light passing through the wooden door which began to illuminate the whole room. I stood still, staring and thinking: "How is it possible that the light goes through the door as if it were made of glass?" Then I saw that she herself passed through the door and

stood right in front of me. It was her! I knelt down. There
was one of the boys sleeping right next to me, so I nudged
him on the foot and said: "Get up; the Virgin came into our
room! Look at her, she's beautiful!"

The boy answered, "Let me sleep. I am tired!" He said it
with a sleepy voice, so I left him alone.

Then I took a good look at her. The light that shone in the
room was coming from a halo of light that enveloped her
whole body. She wore a light blue mantle, crossed at the
shoulder. Her dress was white, long sleeved, pleated over
here [showing]; it was full length. You could only see a little
of her toes. Her face—as I always describe her—was somewhat tanned, her eyes were brown and her hair light brown.
Her head was covered with a white veil toward the back,
under which a bit of hair was showing, so I could see it was
light brown. She also wore a beautiful crown, a queen's
crown, capped by a cross. It had many precious stones and
had the brilliance of gold.

In her arms she was carrying a male Child, about one
year of age. He was slender—not too fat, not too skinny. His
features resembled hers, and His hair was parted to one
side. He wore a cream colored cloak and was covered with
a mantilla, such as those used by cautious and concerned
mothers when their children are small. He would touch his
feet, babble, and smile. When she talked, He would also
speak with His baby talk. The words she said were these:

> *I am very happy with you because you are following
> the inspirations I have given you. I sent you here to
> Our Lady of Victory Church because it is very run
> down, and I want it restored. I desire that the
> Catechism be taught everywhere and that the Word of
> God be proclaimed. I want people to come back to the
> traditions of the Church and to holy water.*

At that moment, I saw, in a small room like ours, a big
church appear. It was large and beautiful. At the main door
there was a holy water font where people would wet their fin-
gers, make the Sign of the Cross and enter to pray before the
sanctuary. Then this vision disappeared, and the room itself
became an enormous church. She continued speaking:

The seventh anniversary of my apparitions in Cuapa is approaching. I want a Solemn Mass to be celebrated in Cuapa and another in this parish of Our Lady of Victory.

She continued:

I want bad books, atheism and communism books, and pornographic magazines burned.

I thought, "This means trouble for me! Who is able to withstand the intellectuals when they say that I am burning books and that such is nonsense!" Thinking of that, I said, "Isn't it wrong to burn books?"

She replied, *"Wrong is to burn the sinner; he can be burned in sin."* Then she looked at the boys asleep with an utterly sweet and maternal look, and said, *"I want them active, diligent, not passive."*

But I kept on thinking: "How am I going to go about buying those books, since I have no money? If I could get money from someone to buy the books, another is going to take it as a good business opportunity, and will start printing more books as I will be buying them to burn them!" I was just thinking, I was not talking!

Then she, who is able to read her children's thoughts, said:

Do not think that you are going to be burning books all of your life. What I want is to leave a symbol by burning whatever books you may find. {She did not say the books you are going to buy, but books that you may find.} *I want it to be a symbol, because the smoke from the burning is going to symbolize the destruction of atheistic communism in Russia and the whole world. I want this symbol to be made.*

She added:

You are going to have problems with some of the priests.

I was very worried because she was announcing trouble and I am tired of having trouble. I thought, "It's enough with the problems I have now, and she is announcing more problems for me? What am I going to do with this? It would be better if she would not tell me this!" But I could not excuse myself.

Sometimes, when I feel that a person comes to talk to me with some unwholesome intention, I will not accept it because the result will be something bad; there is not going to be any good for anybody. In those situations, I take a very negative attitude and I tell the person: "I will not talk with you. Leave me alone!" I am like that, and sometimes I act in a very angry manner, so the person goes away. I am very negative in those cases. But when I feel that what someone is telling me is going to turn into a good thing for the person, for mankind, then I listen and I feel happy. However, I was unable to tell the Virgin that I was feeling uncomfortable about the problems she was warning me about, because it would not have been very polite.

So I said, "What a beautiful child!"

She replied: *"Yes, it is my Son."* She raised the Child moving her arm toward her, and His back was left facing me. Her shoulder was supporting Him. She lifted His robe and I saw the Child's back terribly wounded. It was full of newly made wounds; they were fresh wounds! His flesh was torn in long deep scratches, as if they had been made by a big cat's paws or with a rake. The scratches crisscrossed His back. On His right shoulder there was a big wound, that looked like an open wound, through which the bone was protruding—the bone that moves when one moves the shoulder. Then, pointing to that wound with her left hand, she said:

This is what He suffered because of His love for you all.
I want you to propagate the devotion to the shoulder
wounds of my Son.

I said, "Yes." Then she lowered the Child's robe and placed Him in the position He was before.

What I thought most strange was that the Child did not cry. You know that when a child has any bruise or scratch, he cries, but this One did not cry. He was happy and content. I was dumbfounded!

Then she said, *"If you change and convert, soon, very soon, you will see an end to your sorrows."* Then she added:

Repeat with me this prayer {and she said it slowly}:
*Saint Mary of Victory, Favorite Daughter of God the
Father, give me your faith; Mother of God the Son, give
me your hope; Sacred Spouse of God the Holy Spirit,
give me your charity and cover us with your mantle.
Amen.*

When she said, *"and cover us with your mantle. Amen,"*
I saw myself, and the boys who were sleeping, under a very
fine white web-like fabric, something like an onion's mem-
brane. It was so delicate, so nice that you could stay there
motionless and feel no fatigue or pain after staying in the
same position for a long time. That is what I felt and saw.

Another thing I thought was strange was that I became
insensitive to discomfort. During the next eight days, I did
not feel hot or cold, nor weariness or pain in my legs. I did
not feel any discomfort. I could not become angry. I was not
disturbed by anyone, neither by the seminarians, nor by the
rector, nor by anyone. There is normally something that
gnaws at your inner being, but not at me then. That condition lasted for eight days. I did work. Oh yes, I worked and
did a lot of things, and I thought:

Wow; the Virgin made me whole indeed; I feel no pain
whatsoever! This is great! I'll be able to work all my
life as if I were already in Heaven, doing good for people and the Church.

But when the eight days were over, I started to feel the
rays of the scorching sun, the moments of boredom, weariness, and the annoying boys that would say unpleasant
things about me. I had started to feel my normal emotions
once again.

Now, I understand that the Virgin wanted me on those
days to feel the way I felt so I could sense how it will be
when we are in Heaven, but not here on earth. Here we
have to face challenges, and the one who struggles and
faces the spiritual battle, he is the one who gets the crown.
What crown was I going to get during those days when I felt
no problems at all? I would not have gotten anything. Now
I thank God because I am back to my normal self again.

Otherwise, I would have thought I was already in glory, like an angel on the earth.

Then when she began to depart, she told me:

> *You are to say this prayer* {the one she had just given me} *in private, and on May 8 you are going to make it public.*

It was two months before that date. She knew why the prayer should not be made public beforehand, and now I understand the reason. If the message were immediately publicized, there would be people who would manipulate it. The government people would want to manipulate it. Knowing this would happen, she decided to keep the prayer secret until May. In two months, things became calm. On May 8 of that year I made the prayer public. The prayer was never manipulated.

Finally, she did not say to me, *"I will go now,"* or, *"I will be back,"* as in previous apparitions. This time she motioned her head, turned around and moved toward the door, going through it without opening it. The room became dark.

I turned on the light and went to see the door. The door bars—that is, the wooden sticks I had secured the door with—were still in place. Everything was intact. Then I thought, "Would it be that I left the gates open and people are going to get into the church?" Then I went to check the gate, and it was also locked. It had its two crossbars in place! Then I said to myself, "I'll go check the other door, on the side of the sacristy." Everything was just fine, with no signs of anyone having entered the church!

Now, since I did not understand (there are messages that I do not understand), I thought, "I cannot pass through a closed door, but she can." I went to the priest, my spiritual director, and told him:

> Father, I do not understand these things. First, she passed through the door. Second, the Child had fresh wounds, as if they had just been made, but He was not crying! I want you to explain to me these things.

The priest answered:

Well, I will explain the things that you saw. It is a beautiful message and is consistent with sacred revelation. Look, here in the Bible it says that the Virgin's body is now a glorious body, just like her Son's. Therefore, she can pass through a door, a wall, any solid thing, and she can go into a room without opening the doors, because she is a glorious spirit, like her Son! Then, look, that is what Jesus did when the apostles were hiding for fear of their persecutors. They were inside a house, behind closed doors and Jesus entered.

After reading the Bible passage [*John* 20:19], he continued:

Now, about the little Child who was wounded. We know that Jesus was born, grew up, suffered, and that today He is in His glory. What the Virgin showed you was Jesus as a child, then as an adult, and finally in His glory, as He is now, joyful and happy. He no longer feels pain, that is why you saw Him a happy, smiling Child.

Then he adds:

The small Child is one of the joyful mysteries, Jesus' life as a child. His wounded back shows what Jesus suffered and died when He was an adult. Those are the sorrowful mysteries. And the other part, when the Child was happy, smiling, and joyful, those are the glorious mysteries, because He is already in His glory and cannot suffer any longer. She has showed you the fifteen mysteries of the Rosary, the joyful ones, the sorrowful ones, and the glorious ones.

Then he exclaims:

Oh, Bernardo! I envy you. In a few minutes, the Virgin has given you a theology so rich that I, only because I have studied theology for seven years, can understand. But it has taken me a long time, and she gives it to you in just a few minutes!
Then I said:

O, Father. The Virgin gives me theology, but I do not understand it. I have to get someone to explain to me what the Virgin tells me.

My brother, I have narrated the event of this apparition and some of its details because it is very interesting. I think it is necessary that I have provided some explanation because it is good too for you to know what the Virgin was telling me. That was the message at the Our Lady of Victory Church in El Crucero.

[Bernardo is asked to read the following text about St. Bernard of Clairvaux and the devotion to the Shoulder Wound of Christ, taken from *The Pieta Prayer Booklet,* published by Miraculous Lady of the Roses, Hickory Corners, Michigan. It is very interesting to know that this prayer agrees with the message that the Virgin gave Bernardo in El Crucero. When Bernardo was asked if he had read it before the apparition, he answered, "No, I had not read it. I did read it when the pilgrims from Arlington, Virginia, gave me a booklet with the prayer in it last year, around the month of October 1992. I did not know that St. Bernard had asked this question to the Lord." Bernardo says that the apparition of the Virgin at Our Lady of Victory occurred after midnight on March 8, 1987. In a subsequent conversation with Bernardo, he advised that it was the right shoulder of the Child from which he saw the bone protruding. The booklet provided by the pilgrims was the Spanish version of *The Pieta Prayer Booklet.* They gave it to Bernardo during their pilgrimage to Cuapa in September 1992.]

Here is the excerpt from *The Pieta Prayer Booklet:*

It is related in the annals of the Clairvaux monastery that one day St. Bernard asked our Lord which was His greatest unrecorded suffering, and our Lord answered:

I had on My shoulder, while I bore My cross on the Way of Sorrows, a grievous wound, which was more painful than the others, and which is not recorded by men. Honor this wound with thy devotion, and I will grant thee whatsoever thou dost ask through its virtue and merit. And in regard to those who venerate this wound, I will remit to them all their venial sins, and will no longer remember their mortal sins.

Prayer to the Shoulder Wound of Christ

O most loving Jesus, meek Lamb of God, I, a miserable sinner, salute and worship the most sacred Wound of Thy Shoulder on which thou didst bear thy heavy Cross, which so tore Thy flesh and laid bare Thy bones as to inflict on Thee anguish greater than any wound of Thy most blessed Body. I adore Thee, O Jesus most sorrowful; I praise and glorify Thee, and give Thee thanks for this most sacred and painful Wound, beseeching Thee by that exceeding pain, and by the crushing burden of Thy heavy Cross, to be merciful to me, a sinner, to forgive me all my mortal and venial sins, and to lead me on toward Heaven along the Way of the Cross. Amen.

First Message from Jesus Christ

Miriam: Are there several messages that Jesus has given you? How many are there, and on what dates were they given?

Bernardo: I do not remember very clearly the dates. It is hard for me to remember exact dates, but there are two messages from Jesus. One about hurricane Joan [which hit Nicaragua in October 1985] and another, in which the Lord told me about Purgatory. He did not show it to me; He just talked about Heaven, Purgatory, and Hell.

The one about Purgatory was like this. When the military draft was imposed, I became very worried. Not so much because the boys were going to die physically, for the death of the body is merely the passing of the soul on to a new life, hopefully to be with the Lord and to be spiritually alive. I was not worried about that. What did worry me was that all of us are sinners, aren't we? We have to prepare ourselves for the eternal life, and I thought:

Poor boys, they are going to the war. They go today, but tomorrow they will come back dead, and they have not asked forgiveness for their sins. These boys are going to die in sin and will be condemned.

This was a great worry for me. I wanted to know—just like St. Bernard— what was the destiny that awaited these boys, whether they will be saved or go to Purgatory. I had been taught to pray to my guardian angel, at least one Our Father in the evening, at bedtime. Then I prayed to my guardian angel and said to him:

> Look, I am going to bed now. So, I will not need you because I am not going to be running around. I will be with the Lord and the Virgin. They will accompany me. So, I won't be needing you. Go therefore with the guardian angels of the boys to remind them to remember Jesus and Mary when they are dying, and to ask the Lord forgiveness for their sins. You go together with their guardian angels to do that, and leave me here. {I would always speak this way to him, just like talking to another person}. Go there where the boys are dying, to remind them about the sweet names of Jesus and Mary, so they ask God to forgive their sins so they can be forgiven.

One day I was praying this way (to my guardian angel). I remember it was the day of a martyr saint, January 20, [1984], the day of St. Sebastian. I believed that Msgr. Mondragón was going to celebrate St. Sebastian's Mass at the Calvary Church [in the northeastern portion of Managua]. So that day I got up early and quickly prayed for the boys, because I did want to go to the Calvary Church. I got ready and asked Msgr. Mondragón, "Father, are you going to the Calvary Church?"

"Yes," he said. "I am going to celebrate St. Sebastian's Mass."

"That's very good," I said. He is the patron saint of Acoyapa, a town which is located in Chontales, so I went with him.

I had a pain in my leg so the priest told me: "Do not sit in the pews because it is too crowded. Sit on the steps to the side altar. In the pews, you may hurt your leg. Besides, at the time of the Sign of Peace, many people are going to try to give you the Sign of Peace, and that is disturbing."

I obeyed and located myself on the steps. At the time of the elevation, the priest raised the Host very slowly and solemnly, and at that precise moment, I no longer saw the bread, but a brilliant sun with a bright light shining forth.

Msgr. Mondragón's skin is dark, so his hands looked very dark, almost black against the marvelous light. When he lowered his hands, the Host became visible again. During all the elevation, I could see the brilliance emanating out of the Host and sometimes from the chalice. It was a powerful light. I had already seen this twice before, once at the site of the Cuapa apparitions and another time at a church; the first with my confessor in Cuapa, and the second with Msgr. Francisco Garcia in Granada. And now this third time in the hands of Msgr. Mondragón. "Very well," I said, "see how beautiful it is." I was standing up; I was not allowed to kneel because of my knee ailment. But I felt a strong impulse to kneel, and I did during the consecration.

When it was time for the exchange of the peace greeting, I did not hear the voices of the people, but I began to hear what the Lord was telling me. It was a manly voice from a very majestic Lord, someone utterly respectable. It is hard for me to describe it well. I felt not afraid but aware that it was the Lord that was everything in Himself. The Lord was like the Almighty. I was enraptured listening to the Lord's voice, Who was telling me:

I have heard my Mother's prayers, your prayers, and the boys' prayers. When a lad says, 'I do not want to kill my brother for the sake of the fifth commandment,' which is 'Do not kill,' this is, for the dying lad, like a second baptism. These persons go directly to Heaven, even though they die in the war, because my Mother, you, and other charitable people have prayed for them, for those who are going to die. When a lad or a man does not want to go to war because he does not want to kill his brother and he does want to obey my fifth commandment, if he is killed, that will be for him like a second baptism. Such persons go directly to Heaven.

Talking about the glory of Heaven, the Lord continued:

There is also the destiny of those who benefit from my Mother's prayers, your prayers, and the prayers of the people who pray for the dead. When a lad refuses to go to war so he is not killed, but not with the greater merit of thinking that he does not want to kill his brother because of the Do Not Kill commandment, such a lad loses merit. He is not condemned, but he goes to Purgatory. The ones who go to Heaven are very few. It is like a drizzle compared to the downpour who fall into Purgatory.

There is still the destiny of the ones who are condemned. These are those who go to war swearing angrily, with a spirit of vengeance, anxious to kill, blaspheming against me, against my Mother, and against the saints. These are the ones that go directly to Hell.

I have this great weakness, and my weakness is for this: To see a person who is so charitable with his neighbor that he forgets his own needs in order to care for the other. To whomever does this, I, because of this weakness of mine, cannot deny anything to that person, and I grant whatever he or she may ask.

This is His weakness, He says, to see somebody caring for the needs of others. If many persons like this would care about the salvation of souls, many, very many, would be the ones who would be saved. But these persons who care for the salvation of others are very few; there are not a lot of them.

And the Lord adds:

This is what I feel and I have explained it to you. I have granted you what you wanted to know: the destiny of the boys.

After this, I told my spiritual director: "Father, I have a little money here. I am going to pay for the Masses for the dead, for those who go to the war."

The priest answered, "There is no need for your money. You and I will do it." Any many, many Masses for the dead were said—for those going to the war and for those who were dying there.

I am going to tell you something very sad that happened to me. The Lord gave me visions that seemed so real to me in order to confirm and ratify His message. I saw people very worried and praying for those going to the war. I also saw young men saying, "I am not going to kill my brothers. I do not want to violate the fifth commandment, which is, 'Do Not Kill.'" I heard that from the lads themselves! Young people do not normally think on serious matters; they are not like older people who think sensible things. Youngsters do not go about thinking about the philosophy or wisdom of things. Nonetheless, I saw a boy who said: "No; I won't go because I do not want to kill my brother. I do not want to violate our Lord's fifth commandment, which is, 'Do Not Kill.'" Then, I saw that the lad was standing right next to his father. Then, Bang! Bang! The boy was shot to death. I saw all that. Then I looked and there was another, who said, "Oh, I do not want to go to the war because they are going to kill me!" He was trembling. This boy was also killed, but he failed to say that he did not want to kill his brother and violate the fifth commandment. Now, on the third day, there was yet another young man who said: "I am going to get even and kill those bastards! Wherever I kill them, I'll drink their blood. If I'm hungry, I'll drink a gulp of their blood" (from the dead man's body!). This lad was already uttering words as if he were already in Hell!

Then I said, "Blessed Virgin! Lady, please help him! Poor boy, he's going to go to Hell, because he is full of hatred and is going to kill a fellow man!" I saw all of that. Then, the Lord told me to pay attention to the person's attitude.

Thus, that is the first of the messages the Lord gave me.

Second Message from Jesus Christ

After this and shortly before Hurricane Joan, which passed around the 26th of October 1985, I received another message.

The story begins in early October. You may have learned that everything was rationed in Nicaragua, including gasoline and other products. To obtain gasoline, you needed to buy with coupons, and there were coupons for every vehicle. The parish of Our Lady of Victory had an old pickup truck which did not run, but it still had its registration papers. I used to go by bus to claim the gasoline coupons and gave them to the priest so he could use the gasoline.

But I had to personally go to the Bank of Diriamba [about ten kilometers further south of El Crucero along the south highway that leads from Managua to the border with Costa Rica] to claim the coupons, which were given out once a month.

This time I could not go on a weekday, because I was attending classes, so I went on Saturday, the first Saturday of October of that year [October 5, 1985]. I got on the bus and paid the fare to Diriamba. On my way there I thought, "I am going to pass right in front of Our Lady of Victory Church, and I am not going to stop to greet her!" My normal greeting is to pray three Hail Marys in front of the statue of Our Lady of Victory inside the Church. Then I thought, "Well, I already paid the fare, and if I get off at the church, I'll have to pay again and spend more money." But then I remembered my late grandmother who gave me good advice. She said that you don't go about placing price tags on the Lord's things, nor obstacles or conditions. And I was putting conditions. "Here I have a few cents," I thought. "I can get off, and then I'll pay another fare to go to Diriamba. No stinginess with the Lord!" I decided to get off. The bus stopped right in front of the church. I got off, opened the gate, and after locking it back up, I entered the church.

I prayed the three Hail Marys in the presence of the Virgin. Since it was pretty early (before the next bus came), I wanted to just sit for a while. Then, I began to hear a voice like the one I had heard at the Church of Calvary. The voice was saying:

I am very angry because I have seen that my people are suffering greatly. I am going to chastise those who are oppressing my people.

This was repeated three times. Then I asked, "Lord, when is this going to happen?"
"Soon, I am going to punish them."
Then I said, "Lord, the Virgin has promised a lot of things and they have not been fulfilled. (I do not know why I said that to the Lord. Bishop Bosco Vivas tells me it was a mistake to have said this, but, then, sometimes the Lord gets good out of people's mistakes. Everything the Virgin has said to me has been fulfilled! So, I don't know why I said it.)

He did not answer me and then said, *"But I am going to punish those who oppress my people, because I am tired of seeing them suffer."*

I asked, "When is this going to be, Lord?"

"Soon," He replied. But, seeing that I insisted on knowing when, and that I did not seem satisfied with the response, He said, *"Don't you believe in Him Who made the sun stop?"*

I said, "Yes, Lord, I believe!"

"Well, then, the same One that made the sun stop is going to punish those who oppress His people."

"When is this going to be?" I asked.

"Soon. I want you to ask for it!" {the punishment}.

At that moment I felt so small, so insignificant, so lacking in merit! I felt like an ant, an insect, incapable of doing anything. I said: "But Lord, You know everything, and You see everything. I only see what goes on around me. It is true that I can see around me those who are suffering, but You can see everywhere. You see all of Your children. What I see is but a little circle of the suffering; You see the whole world, and You can do it without my asking for it!"

The Lord said:

No, this is how I want it. Let Heaven and earth unite in this request.

(That is why sometimes, when I give a talk, I tell the people that the Lord wants us to ask. Because He is our Father, He wants us to ask for things.)

When I said to the Lord, "You can do it," He replied,

Elijah was a man just like you, and he prayed that no rain might fall, and it did not rain. Then he prayed for the rain to fall, and it did [James 5:17; 1 Kings 17:1-17; 18:42-45]. This is how I want you to do it.

I had already read about Elijah, so I asked, "How am I supposed to pray?"

He told me:

You are going to say: "Lord, let Your curse fall upon the oppressors of Your people. But let this curse become a a blessing for Your people." That is the way I want you to ask for it.

I then said: "Lord, are you going to punish the people of Managua? And those of El Crucero? Poor people!"

He replied: *"No, nothing is going to happen here."*

But I insisted: "Lord, but Your punishment falls on everyone, not just the bad! Then there is going to be punishment for innocent people." I did not want innocent people to suffer the chastisement, because I could sense that a terrible, horrifying thing was going to happen. I had that feeling!

Then he said:

It is true that my chastisements fall on everyone, but it is the last thing they are going to suffer. I will have the innocent in my kingdom, and I will punish the others.

Then I again asked him: "Lord, I want to know the day and the hour this is going to happen."

He said:

Now, that you are going to Diriamba {I had not told anybody I was going to Diriamba} *you are going to receive something white, white as a jasmine* [a white flower].

Then I asked, "Is someone going to give me a flower, a white rose?

He said, *"No,"* and with that "no," the dialogue finished.

I left the church full of joy. I do not remember how I got to Diriamba, because I was so happy. I was not aware of what I was doing. I don't even know if I paid a new fare. I just got on a bus.

When I got to Diriamba, I went to the bank. The guard told me that the bank was now closed on Saturdays; it was open only Monday through Friday, so I had to come back on Monday. Well, normally, when things do not work out the way I expect, it bothers me a lot. I get very disturbed. That day, however, I was feeling a sweet joy inside. It was like the meekness of a dove.

In Diriamba, I used to visit only two families, because I don't like to be too conspicuous. I prefer not to be noticed, so people don't say, "Look, there goes Bernardo!" and then ask me about the messages right on the street. I prefer to talk with the people at a meeting and explain everything well.

The two families that I normally visit in Diriamba are Señora Ines' and the Parrales' families. They are very good people. Señora Ines is an old lady who calls me, "My little boy!" and she gets very happy when she sees me.

That day she told me, "Bernardo, Cecilia wants to see you."

Oh, Señora Ines," I exclaimed, why did you tell her that I was coming here? I don't like to be going from one place to another. I like to go unnoticed!"

She replied smiling, "Cecilia already knows you. She wants to tell you about a miracle the Virgin did for her. By a miracle she was spared from an operation!"

I am interested in certificates about illnesses, especially when a doctor certifies that a disease is incurable and then the patient is healed miraculously. I am interested in the certification in order to obtain the approval for the miracles. A number of documents have to be gathered, because there are investigations that have to be made for the approval, and miracles have to be documented. So I need those certificates to take them to the church.

"Let's go for a while," I answered because I had to return to the seminary.

Cecilia already knew me after all. "Hi, Bernardo," she greeted me. A man came in after her and she introduced me to him saying, "This is Bernardo." (I signaled Cecilia to be quiet.)

"Sure, I already met him," the man said, shaking my hand. "I am now going to the United States, so I have to go take a shower."

"Have a good trip," I said, and he went to take a shower because he had been to the beach.

When he left, the man was carrying a white cap in his hand; it was very, very white. He said, "Bernardo, do you like to wear caps?" (because I was wearing a cap). "I am going to give you this one."

Immediately I thought, "This is the sign." But I could not tell anyone, because first I had to tell my spiritual director.

I saw that the cap did not have any label as they usually do, so I put it on my head, and Celilia said: "He looks great! Don't you have a camera to take his picture?" Then the man took my picture and said, "I am going to develop it in the United States."

"When he brings the picture, I'd like to have one. Please, ask him to give me a copy," I asked Cecilia.

Now, I have the picture where I am wearing that cap. I left the house and went to drop by Señora Ines' home. After that, I left for the Parrales' home. I took off the white cap and put on the old one. Upon my arrival, they asked me, "Who gave you that cap?"

"Cecilia's son-in-law," I answered. (But I haven't even met the man before; it was the first time I saw him!) The Parrales sisters gave me a plastic bag to carry the cap. Monsignor told me to keep the cap in remembrance of this message.

That was the message.

Twenty-two days later, Hurricane Joan came. I was not scared, so I went to comfort some relatives of mine that were very frightened because of the hurricane. I told them: "Pray to the Blessed Virgin. Pray the Rosary and go to sleep. Don't think that something is going to happen to you."

And so it was; nothing happened to them. In Managua, the hurricane went by as a tropical storm, and at El Crucero it wasn't even windy. I was very happy that nothing had happened to the poor people in El Crucero because, oh, my God!, the wind sweeps the huts away and the poor people lose absolutely everything! Then I thought how bad it could have been for poor Managua! But look, it was wonderful! The hurricane lost its eye behind the Amerrisque mountain range in the Cuapa district before reaching Managua. It passed through Managua as a tropical storm, with a light tropical rain, and then it became a hurricane again over the Pacific. There, its name became Miriam, and finally it died down.

See what the Lord did! The hurricane, as it passed behind the Amerrisque mountain range, lost its eye. Then it passed over Cuapa, headed in the direction of Managua, then it went through Managua as mere tropical rain. Then it rebuilt itself again and it became hurricane Miriam—first Joan and then Miriam. Even the names coincide! It coincides with St. Joan of Arc. As Msgr. Mondragón, my spiritual director, said: "Look! That is St. Joan of Arc who has been striking the Sandinistas with her sword!" And so it was.

[In a subsequent conversation, Bernardo explained that Miriam is Hebrew for Mary. And as St. Joan of Arc had freed France, she and the Blessed Mother were freeing Nicaragua from the Sandinistas. For a further understanding of Bernardo's statement, see Bernardo's dream with St. Joan of Arc. It is item #18 near the end of Part II.]

In the Sandinista military bases there was great destruction, and from then on their downfall began. They became weaker and weaker until it culminated with the election won by Señora Chamorro. [Violeta Barrios de Chamorro was elected President of Nicaragua on February 25, 1990, in what was a stunning defeat to the Sandinista leadership and a shock to most of the world's press.]

This is the second message given to me personally by the Lord. The other messages I received were given to me by the Virgin Mary.

Miriam: Which hurricane was this one?

Bernardo: It was called Hurricane Joan on the Atlantic coast. I realized it was coming before it happened, so I told the priests about it. We were sure that nothing was going to happen in Managua, nor in El Crucero. They know about it because I told them.

Father told me, "You keep your cap; do not give it away nor wear it." So, what I have is a relic. People have asked me to give it to them, but I won't. "Monsignor told me not to give it away," I tell them. I also keep the door the Virgin went through when I saw her at El Crucero. We had to remove it and put it away because people were breaking pieces off it in order to make relics so each one could have a piece of the door!

Questions on Various Subjects

1. MEANING OF CUAPA

Miriam: Did you know, before the 1980 apparitions, what was the meaning of the name of Cuapa in the native Indian Guajin dialect?

Bernardo: It is in the Nahuatl native Indian language. I did not know it. I am going to tell you about a vanity that I used to have. When I was young, I said: "Cuapa! What a horrible name! I don't like it!" Young people always have their pretensions, don't they? When I was asked where was I from, I replied, "From Juigalpa." [Juigalpa is the capital city of the Chontales Department. It is about 25 kilometers from Cuapa. It took Bernardo four hours to walk from Cuapa to Juigalpa.] But I did not then know the meaning of the name Cuapa.

Now, after the apparitions, some research has been made about this. The historical archives of Nicaragua were lost at some point. The archives where Cuapa is mentioned are in Guatemala, the antiquities archives, where they have been keeping the documents and records on the indigenous traditions, documents on the historical origins, and so on. You all know that we (Nicaraguans) are somewhat careless, that we do not keep our own historical evidences, because maybe we do not appreciate them, and do not care about some really beautiful things that we have. And this is a beautiful thing.

So, in the Guatemala archives there are references to Cuapa, the way the town used to be. When you separate the syllables of the word Cuapa, as it is now in Spanish, you have CUA and PA: "CUA" means "snake or serpent" and "PA" means "on." Even now we utilize this native expression, because when kids are playing and they get into a fight and one of them hits the other, one of the women in the neighborhood says: "That boy . . . is going to be a jerk! PA!, he hit the other on the head with a club!" This PA! word we use is heard mostly among the humble people, the less learned. Then, I say, "Can you see? PA is still being used!" It means "on."

So, Cuapa means that the serpent's head was crushed with

a blow! And, who did it? The Blessed Virgin Mary of course! Now, I repent for having belittled my own birthplace, because now I know how great it is, what I used to despise. But it was because of ignorance that I rejected my own home town when I said that I was from Juigalpa and not from Cuapa.

[We personally find intriguing this particular historical interpretation of the native Nahuatl language on the meaning of "Cuapa" (as it is presently spelled in modern Spanish). We are not knowledgeable about the various Indian languages, including Nahuatl, which were spoken by the inhabitants of what now constitutes Mexico, Nicaragua, or Venezuela. There is no doubt, however, that in the apparition of the Blessed Virgin Mary in early December 1531, on the outskirts of what was to become Mexico City, to Juan Diego, who did not speak Spanish, their communication was in the native language of this Indian peasant, which was some dialect of Nahuatl. The Bishop, a Spaniard, through his Indian translator, interpreted the name Our Lady gave to Juan Diego as "Lady of Guadalupe," which makes good sense because at that time (c. 1500) there was a famous and popular Marian shrine back in Spain under that title. In fact, Christopher Columbus, after one of his return voyages, made a pilgrimage to that shrine to thank the Blessed Mother. However, the name the Blessed Mother actually conveyed to Juan Diego was communicated in his native Nahuatl dialect. Guadalupe can be broken down into these two phonetic parts, "Guadalu" and "pe." (Apparently, Nahuatl has no "g" or "d" sound.) These parts sound a lot like "Cua - pa." Whether there is any connection here, we will have to leave to the Nahuatl linguistic experts. But in view of the role "serpents" played in the religious beliefs of the native Indians of Central America, and that one of their primary gods was "Quetzalcoatl," the "feathered serpent," representing in their religious myth sort of an incarnation of the sky (bird = "quetzal") with the land (snake = "coatl"), it would not be surprising if Our Lady described herself, in part, to Juan Diego as "I am the one who crushed the head of the serpent." Such a title, if it had been given, would carry special significance to the pagan Indian culture, coming within ten years after the defeat of the Aztecs by Cortez (a catastrophe of truly "biblical" magnitude for the native Indian culture in Central America) as well as to the Christian Spanish community (the "women" in *Genesis/Revelation*—the alpha and omega books of the Christian Bible). Would such a duality of meaning in the message from Heaven to these now joined cultures be more far fetched than the use of Spanish Castilian roses in early December in mile high terrain (i.e., the Mystical Rose) to create the miraculous image on the tilma (cloak) of Juan Diego of a dark (olive) skinned pregnant Indian princess of high royalty (i.e., the Ark of the New Covenant)? For what it may be worth, the apparition of the Blessed Mother to Maria Esperanza de Bianchini during the past two decades, which have been approved by the local Venezuelan bishop, have taken place on her farm, which is known as Betania. Betania, however, is located in a district of Venezuela named "Cua." Whether there is any possible similarity here in the native Indian language, we do not know. Finally, it was interesting to see in the courtyard of the Pater Noster Church, the church which commemorates Christ's teaching His Apostles the "Our Father" and which is located on the Mount of Olives (the place from which Christ ascended into Heaven) in Jerusalem, Israel, that among the many languages from around the world in which the text of the "Our Father" is represented on its walls, there is a plaque containing the "Our Father" in Nahuatl.]

2. BERNARDO'S CHILDHOOD

Bernardo: I was born in Cuapa on August 20, 1931 [the feast of St. Bernard of Clairvaux]. My mother's name was Simeona. She was a housewife. She did her housework, embroidery, sewing, and everything else at home. My father's name was Baltazar. He was a farmer and he would sell his produce in Santo Domingo and La Libertad. My father's complexion was dark, just like the Negro people of the Nicaragua coast lands. He was elegant, tall, but a little dark complected. My grandmother's family was light skinned, green-eyed, very elegant. My father and my mother fell in love, but my grandmother did not approve of it, because she said that he was "black," and she did not like the idea of her daughter being married to a "black man." But you know that love sees no colors or sizes or anything else. No question about it. They loved each other.

My father promised to marry my mother and to take her away. At that time, you had to go to Juigalpa on horseback. One night they eloped. Since both of them were adults, he arranged everything, looked for the judge and the priest, and they got married. [Unlike in the United States where the priest serves as the official representative of both the Church and the State, in Nicaragua the priest represents only the Church. It is, therefore, necessary to also be married by a civil judge, which constitutes the legal marriage under Nicaraguan law.] Then my grandmother became angry with her daughter and her son-in-law. My father and my mother set up their own home, but they could not go to my grandmother's because she would have dealt them PA! (a club blow on their heads). One year later, a baby boy was born. It was I, and I was not as dark skinned as my father. My grandmother's sister came to see her grandnephew and returned to tell my grandmother: "You should see the baby boy! He is so cute! He does not look like his dad; he is like his mom!" Then my grandmother went to see her daughter. So I was the cause for the reconciliation between them, because when I was born, mother, daughter, and son-in-law got back together.

But, when my grandmother saw me, she said to herself: "This is my son! He is not that black man's son!" My mother thought my grandmother was joking, because they were friends again. So she went to the kitchen to prepare dinner. My father was at work. My mother went on talking from the kitchen, but when she realized that no one was talking back to her she went to see where her mother was. What a shock when she realized that neither her mother nor her child were there! She ran down the road, but could not even see her mother, who was carrying me in her arms, because her mother had too much of a head start. My mother did not want to go to her mother's house because she feared that her mother would punish her and take revenge for all that had happened before. Then, my mother, overcome with grief, cried a lot.

When my father came home she told him everything and that she did not have the baby. My father was a very calm, understanding man, so he said: "Don't cry. Let her have the baby. When the boy cries at night asking for food he will annoy her; she will become desperate, and will end up bringing him here." But my grandmother was a stubborn lady. She did not take me back to my mother, and she fed me regular cow's milk.

My father had not yet gone to the Civil Registrar's Office in

Juigalpa to register me. Then my grandmother said: "Well, this baby is going to be mine and my husband's son. He will be registered with our family name." My father's last name was Urbina and my mother's Martinez. My grandmother's maiden name was Jaime and her husband's was Martinez. So she registered me under my grandparents' names. That was how I got to grow up with her during all my childhood. But I did go to see my real parents.

My parents moved to the mountains, further away from my grandmother's house. I called her "Mom," but she always told me, "I am not your mother; I am your Granny. I raised you, but you have your own mother. You have a Mother in Heaven and the other on the mountains." She did not deprive me from my parents' love; she always raised me with this kind of love. I used to go to see them in the mountains, but then I would return to my grandmother's house because that was where I wanted to be. I was very happy.

When I grew up, my grandmother used to tell me: "Son, a man has to get married and set up a home. You have to work; you have to be a real man." I had my friends, boys and girls, and she used to tell me, "Be careful with girls. Don't hurt them. You have to choose one, the one you like the best, so you can marry her."

"Yes," I replied jokingly, "I am going to choose a very pretty one, Granny." She would advise me, "Ask St. Joseph, the friend and protector of the young, so he can choose a good wife for you." She taught me a prayer to him:

> *Oh, Saint Joseph, you were particularly obedient to the inspirations of the Holy Spirit. Grant me the grace of knowing the state that Divine Providence has destined me for. Oh, foster father of Jesus, friend and protector of the young, grant me the light to know the Divine Will and strength to follow it, so I can enter and persevere on the road that will lead me to eternal happiness. Amen.*

She taught me this prayer so I would become a devout son of his, so he, as protector of the young, would choose a good girl to be my wife.

Miriam: Bernardo, how many brothers and sisters do you have?

Bernardo: We are three sisters and three brothers. I am the oldest one. The second one is Marina, the next is Celia, and my third sister is Leonor; they are all alive. My brothers are Jose Luis and Basiliso. Basiliso was also the name of one of my mother's uncles.

3. BERNARDO'S SCHOOLING

Miriam: Did you go to school in Cuapa?

Bernardo: I went to high school in Cuapa.

When I was younger, they took me to church. I wanted to be a priest, because I thought everything priests did and said was beautiful. But my grandmother used to tell me that "a son of a scorpion cannot become a cockroach." She said this because my grandfather was somewhat of a womanizer as was my father. My grandfather had left my grandmother for another woman, so she would tell me: "Like father, like son! How is it that a good priest is going to come from womanizing fathers? Yours is going to be a bad priesthood! I think that you'll be just like them. The difference is that you know how to conceal it!" She was a distrustful person.

At about that time, I left home. I was 14 years old. I went on a truck to Granada. I learned how to read when I stayed for four years studying my grammar education with the Jesuits in Granada. I was treated as if I were a member of their family. The school, Centroamerica, was next to Lake Nicaragua. They loved me a lot and taught me how to become a tailor, and also some of the skills of an electrician, bricklayer, and plumber. That is why now I insist that Nicaraguan schools should teach manual trades, something practical for boys and girls to get work when they leave school. We have to work, not only learn the theories. Sometimes it is hard to find work. But if you know a trade, you can earn your living.

Miriam: Do you mean that you stayed with the Jesuits for four years?

Bernardo: Yes. After that I went to Juigalpa to finish grammar school, that is the fifth and sixth grades. Then I came back to Cuapa, to take care of my grandmother, who was elderly, until she died [on June 5, 1974]. Later, I continued to study and I finished my first three years of high school education in 1978. [Bernardo subsequently advised that he completed his last two years of high school in1989.]

4. BERNARDO'S OCCUPATIONS

Miriam: Did you work? How did you support yourself?

Bernardo: I worked as a tailor. But my employment has often changed. At first, I used to work on farms with the machete, sowing beans, corn, rice. I am familiar with farm work. I used to work from 6 a.m. to 6 p.m., just like a man, even though I was still a boy. I supported my home; I mean that I was just like the head of the house. That is why I say that all my life I have been like the head of the house or the boss at work. I am not used to being ordered around, and it bothers me when someone tries to "manipulate" me and when I am under someone else's authority. I have always been like the head of the house, and that is why people say I am prideful. I know how to milk cows with my own hands and cure animals. I know how to use the lasso, wash animals, and everything. Later on, I worked as a tailor. I also liked a lot teaching boys and girls, and many of them learned the tailor and dressmaking trades, and now they earn their living. I, like St. Paul, have spiritually begotten children, who are now making a living even in the United States. They are supporting themselves with what they learned from me.

5. BERNARDO'S VISITS TO THE UNITED STATES

Miriam: How many times have you been to the United States?

Bernardo: This is the third time. [Bernardo subsequently visited us again in October 1994.] The first one I went from Miami to Pittsburgh, in 1991. In 1992, I went from Miami to Los Angeles, and now I have come here to Washington.

Miriam: Have you ever received a locution outside of Nicaragua?

Bernardo: No, I haven't. The first time I came to the States, I went back to Miami from Pittsburgh, and I stayed at a Cuban lady's home. Her name war Irma Campos. She and her nun friend took me to the airport in a taxi cab that had dark tinted windows. Suddenly, I saw something light up inside the cab, something like a glowing piece of satin cloth that was shining with a bluish brilliance. I was riding next to the driver, but I thought, "These ladies are carrying something that glows," and I looked around in the cab to see what it was that was shining, but I saw nothing. They were talking to each other. Then, I lowered the window and saw that there was a cloud in the sky in the shape of a blue mantle spread out in the sky. I kept on looking when the taxicab stopped at a red light. Then, the nun asked me, "What are you looking at? Do you have these kinds of trees in Nicaragua?"

"Yes," I said. "One is an almond tree, but I don't remember what kind of tree is the other one. But I am not looking at the trees. What caught my eye was the glow of that luminous cloud over there!"

They looked up and saw it too. Then they told the driver to stop the cab and stepped out to take some snapshots of the glowing cloud. After processing the film, the image of the Virgin Mary appeared there! That was the only manifestation in the sky that I saw in this country. "This is wonderful," I thought. "It is like a mystery, that the pictures taken by Doña Irma and Sister Rosa Delfina with their own cameras showed the image, but the picture taken by the cab driver with his camera did not show anything special, only the dark sky."

6. Acquisition of Illuminating Statue for Cuapa

Miriam: We want to ask you about the statue that you liked so much when you were a boy. How old were you at that time?

Bernardo: Okay. That statue of the Blessed Virgin was in Juigalpa. It is of the old kind, those which they used to dress up. Now statues are not dressed up. I was about eight years old. [This would make it sometime c. 1939.] At that time I used to say that I was going to marry a very beautiful woman, one who would be only for me, and I said so to my grandmother. She told me that I did nothing but think nonsense.

One day we went to the church in Juigalpa. After Mass, while my grandmother stayed talking to some friends of hers, I began looking at the images in the church. I thought that statues were like living persons since they were big. I came in front of the statue of Our Lady of Mount Carmel and thought, "This one is married, although her husband is not here, but since she has her child, she is married." Then, "Look how beautiful this other one is!" I thought when looking at the Holy Family where St. Joseph, the Virgin Mary, and the Christ Child were together. "This one is married and her husband is here. What a beautiful wife this man has!" I was admiring all the statues of the Virgin. I then came to where there was an image of St. Anthony and thought, "This one is a married man. He has a handsome child, but his wife is not here. Maybe she is taking care of their home." Next, I came to this particular statue which was in her own niche, and thought, "This one is alone, she is single. This is the one I am going to marry. All the other ones are already married, but this one, who is also very pretty, is the one I am going to marry." I went back home thinking that the statue was a real person!

In Cuapa, a lady from the neighborhood would tell me that I was going to marry her daughter—that she was my fiancée—and she made the girl believe that I was her fiancé. This is a custom or tradition people have in Nicaragua. When this lady came to our house one day, she told my grandmother, "This is the girl, Señora Martinez, Bernardo's fiancée."

The girl was very well groomed and all dressed up. I stared at the poor girl and said: "Lady, your daughter is ugly! I am going to marry a very beautiful young woman I saw in Juigalpa."

"Where did you see such a pretty girl?" the lady asked me. (She was not offended at my saying that her daughter was ugly!)

"Well, Granny and I went to this huge old house, and there on the walls there were these little places with room only for the wife, the husband, or the child. There I saw a very beautiful girl, and that is the one I am going to marry!" I replied.

"Crazy boy!" exclaimed my grandmother, "that is the

Virgin Mary. You are talking nonsense!"

"In my surprise, I kept quiet. I felt a great love for the Virgin, and every time I would go to Juigalpa, I went to visit her. I only looked at that statue, because I already knew it was the Virgin Mary, and I would think: "She is beautiful! It is true that if I could marry her, I would, even though she is the Virgin!"

Fr. Octavio Mejía Vilchez was the pastor of that church for 15 years. He had a strange illness that had attacked his knees and sometimes he would fall to the floor, so he had to walk leaning on a cane. Besides that, all of a sudden he would become very irritable. He was a good man, a nice person, but when he was feeling bad, he was terrible!

One day [several years later, when Bernardo was 14 years of age] he asked me, "Are you coming to the procession we are going to have?"

"Which one?" I asked.

"The Daughters of Mary are going to buy a new statue from Barcelona, in Spain—a modern one, very pretty. We are going to replace this one we have now, because you cannot have two images in the same church, and we are going to have a procession from El Salto [about 2.5 kilometers from Juigalpa] up to Juigalpa. You are invited to join us."

I thanked him and asked, "What are you going to do with this old image?"

"I don't know what to do with it," he replied. "Nobody wants it; not even as a gift! And you cannot have two statues in the same church." Then he told me that it would probably be burned.

This came to me like a dagger piercing my heart and I felt so sad. Burn the statue of the Virgin Mary? The one I was in love with? Then I said to him, "Father, can't you sell it?"

He said he would sell it for 300 córdobas. [This is 300 córdobas, "Nicaraguan" dollars. The conversion rate historically has been around 7 córdobas equals one U.S. dollar. Hence, this would be approximately $40 in U.S. money, which still was a small fortune for a Nicaraguan lad 14 years old in 1945.]

"Okay," I said. "If we can buy it, we will buy it, because we don't have one."

In Cuapa I told the people, mainly the adults, that we

should buy the statue, because otherwise they were going to burn it, and I told them everything Father Mejía had told me. But they would not listen. Now I think the adults did not do right in this. Sometimes they do not consider the concerns of the young people, when those concerns are good. It is true that many times boys and girls need to be corrected, but they disregarded my request. Then I gathered my friends, boys and girls, and suggested the idea of buying the statue ourselves. We formed a sort of committee and prepared a notebook to record the names of the contributors and the amounts of money donated to buy the statue of the Virgin Mary. We also wrote in the notebook a short introduction and the names of the persons who would be collecting the contributions.

Next Sunday, we all went out together to raise money. The people would give five or ten cents. Some would give willingly, others grudgingly. Some would welcome the idea, others would reject it. They said: "Lazy rascals! They are only getting money so they can buy shirts for themselves!" This reaction made a very negative impact on some of the young people, so many quit participating in our committee. Moreover, some parents did not allow their sons or daughters to continue their involvement because they said we would steal the money. Only a tiny group of girls remained with myself, the only boy. Finally, we were able to collect the 300 córdobas, and I took them to Father to buy the statue.

Fr. Mejía received the money with joy, and I asked him to write me a receipt. He did, signed and sealed it, and gave it to me. I still keep it in the archives of the Cuapa Parish. He asked me to take away the statue of the Virgin before the new one arrived. There was no one who would help me take the image from Juigalpa to Cuapa, so I ended up asking my uncle-in-law to help me. He agreed and told me to prepare another horse (at that time this road was traveled on horseback) with pillows and a blanket to wrap the statue. When we got to a place called Plan de la Piedra, we put the image on our shoulders and began a procession. [Plan de la Piedra is the name of a gigantic monolith rock that is approximately 5 kilometers southwest of Cuapa. This rock is visible from all over the Cuapa area. Bernardo enjoyed climbing it as a youth.] The arrival of the Virgin

Mary was very solemn. Once in Cuapa, we installed the statue in the church. The priest had given us the old altar, and a man named Gabriel Raudes took it to Cuapa, charging us 100 córdobas for the service. Cuapa is 25 kilometers from Juigalpa, so this Señor Raudes made the entire trip on foot carrying the altar on his shoulders.

Now when the statue became illuminated and appeared to be alive, the people from Juigalpa wanted to get it back, but then I showed them the receipt and told them: "You have no right to claim it. You did not want it and we do appreciate her! So, the Virgin has to be in a place where she is appreciated!"

This is the story of the statue of the Blessed Virgin Mary.

Miriam: Thank you. It is beautiful story. And after such a big effort to get it, the Virgin made her first miracle becoming illuminated. How tall is the statue?

Bernardo: About 4 feet tall.

Miriam: What is it made of?

Bernardo: It is made of cedarwood. It is an old image. Normally the sculptor or carver signs his name at the base of a statue, but there is no name on this one. It is old, and that is why the people did not want it.

Miriam: How long has it been in the Cuapa church?

Bernardo: Over 20 years. [Actually, it was closer to 35 years by the time the statue illuminated in April 1980.]

Miriam: How long was it at the Juigalpa church?

Bernardo: Since it was made—I don't remember. Sr. Clement, who used to take wildflowers to the Virgin and who is now elderly, remembers who carved it. We believe that the statue is over 100 years old.

Miriam: When you bought the statue, how old were you, Bernardo?

Bernardo: I was fourteen.

Miriam: We can see in the picture that the Virgin has a dress. Who provided the clothes for her?

Bernardo: The Daughters of Mary provided them. At first she had a dress box, just like a person who travels from one place to another, but later her clothes began deteriorating. After the community of the Daughters of Mary disappeared from the Cuapa parish, I was the one who would buy clothes for her with my own money. When the statue became illuminated, she was wearing a green dress. I gave this dress to Mother Paula in exchange for another very pretty dress that she gave me for the Virgin. [Sister Paula Hildalgo is a close friend of Bernardo. She is currently teaching in a school for poor children in Managua.]

7. LOCUTION FROM THE VIRGIN CONCERNING TEACHING VOCATIONAL SKILLS

Miriam: We would like to know about the locutions you received from the Blessed Virgin.

Bernardo: Well, I would have to tell you just the most important ones, because they are many.

Miriam: When you hear a locution, do you hear the voice inside or outside of you? How do you recognize the voice? Could you describe it?

Bernardo: Well, I do not hear an inner voice. I hear her voice as if she was hiding behind something and I could only hear her voice. For instance, if there is a person in the room next door talking to me, I can recognize his or her voice. This is what I would compare it to. But I do recognize the sound of her voice, and my heart fills with joy, even though she may be announcing problems to me. I feel so happy! This is how I felt last Wednesday, the 13th of January [1993].

I had the idea of organizing an art school in El Crucero, where different kinds of art would be taught, and tablecloths and ornaments could be made for the church. I asked a lady if she could teach art classes for boys and girls on

Saturdays maybe, as a beginning. This way I could gather more resources and money so we could establish the art school and also provide classes for homemakers, because there is a great need in this area. I went to El Crucero to talk to this lady and show her where the classes could be held, so we could start as soon as possible. On my way back, I was riding on the back of a pickup truck, when I heard "Her" voice telling me:

You are working in things that I approve, because that is what I want for the poorest of my children. For some it is easier, but not for others, and nobody cares for them. I am concerned about that. When I was on the earth, I used to teach girls to sew, because I knew how to do it. My immaculate husband Joseph used to do the same, too. He would teach the Boy Jesus the carpenter's trade, so He could earn His own living, and he also used to teach other boys. This is what I want. I am very happy with what you are doing. But not everything is going to be glorious and joyful; you will also have times of sadness and problems, and you will suffer a great deal because of this. You will find opposition, and people will say that you made up all of this nonsense. But you will succeed. Do not despair; rejoice because you will do good for many people. You will have problems and sufferings, some even caused by priests. If they do not allow you to work, then do it in your own house, even in Cuapa.

I still own some 15 acres of land in that area (Cuapa). I already gave four acres to the Church, at the place where she appeared. I felt very happy, even though she was announcing to me many problems. I still felt very happy. I was listening to all of this while riding on the pickup truck on my way back from El Crucero to Managua. I was happy thinking that St. Joseph had taught the Child Jesus to use His own hands so He could earn His living, that he taught some other boys too, and that the Virgin Mary would teach other girls of her time. Even knowing there would be problems, I was so happy that, on my way, I started to sing a song my grandmother had taught me:

Some wander the earth in search of happiness,
but not those like I who already possess it;
It flourishes in my heart, not like a wilting flower,
but like an early-blooming rose of perpetual spring.

This was the last locution I have had. It was a very short locution on the day before leaving for the United States. I want to go ahead with the idea of the school, so we can do what our Mother, the Virgin Mary, and her husband used to do.

8. Locution Concerning Our Lady's Future Victory in Nicaragua

Miriam: Did you receive any locutions especially for Nicaragua?

Bernardo: Yes, but is too long. I don't know if you want to listen to it.

Miriam: Among the locutions, is there one that you consider very important?

Bernardo: For me almost all of them are important. One locution for Nicaragua was very beautiful. I can't remember dates very well, but they are recorded in the documents I have written. It was when there was the Marian Congress in Nicaragua, after a whole year of preparations. [The special Marian Year ran from the feast of Pentecost 1987 (June 7) through the Feast of the Assumption 1988 (August 15).] The events in Cuapa had been forgotten. Nobody would talk about Cuapa any more. There were no pilgrimages or anything else. One day I thought, "What a pity. Nobody talks about Cuapa, not even the priest or the bishops. Nobody!"

So, I went to complain about this to Msgr. Bosco Vivas, and he told me, "Well, you have to start doing something."

"Me? How? Doing what?" I thought.

Things stayed the same. Later on I kept on thinking about this and said to myself, "I am at fault too." I am the one who runs things at Our Lady of Victory because there is no priest there. The Nuncio [the Papal Nuncio from the Vatican, Msgr. Pablo Giglio] comes only to celebrate Mass. "Maybe I could ask Monsignor to allow me to paint some letters on the St.

Joan of Arc banner reading, 'Praise Jesus and Mary!' I thought that he would give me permission, because I am like the pastor there, I run the parish. I will put up a sign reading, 'Praise Jesus and Mary!' on the arch above the gate, so at least people can read what it says." Then I thought, "I need some paint. Oil-based paint is the best, but I don't have any money to buy even a pint. Well, I'll have to beg for it. I need just a little, to paint those letters."

I went to see the sisters at the Seminary, and they told me they had paint in several colors, but not white as I wanted. I went to see two painters, but they told me they did not have any. "Oh, my God," I said, "many people offer to help, but nobody gives me any white paint, and I don't have money to buy any!" It was the 1st of August, the day of Saint Dominic's in Managua, a holiday, so I decided to go to the church to clean it. I started doing some cleaning when I noticed a discarded black canister on top of the Virgin's niche. "Somebody put this here just to annoy me," I thought. I took it from there. It was an old, rusty can. It felt heavy too! I opened the top, and, lo and behold, it contained fresh white paint! It was just like new, but the can was old! Wow, I couldn't believe it!

So immediately I started to paint the sign. People passing by would read and say, "See what it says: 'Praise Jesus and Mary.'"

A handicapped man passed by in a wheelchair and he cursed the sign. Then I prayed for his conversion, because he was a renegade. I prayed and finished painting the last letter.

I don't know what happened to me then, because I started seeing all people very skinny, even bony. I thought, "Oh,my God. This paint got me drugged!" It was terrible the way I saw people. I poured water on my head, hoping that the feeling would go away, and then I went to the house where I dine. There were a few girls here, and they greeted me happily. To me they looked normal, well fed. But when I looked at other people, I saw them so strange that I thought I was groggy because of the paint. I went back to the church and into the sacristy to stay there until such a horrible reaction would fade away.

After a while I heard the horn of a truck. It was Mauricio, a big, fat young man, but I saw him skinny, ugly! I asked him what he wanted, and he said, "Monsignor Andino just died, and Father wants you to come."

I had not lost my mind after all, so I went to the sisters and told them we were going to have a vigil service for Monsignor at the Seminary. I made arrangements to have the church prepared and to hold the burial service in the El Crucero cemetery. I made decisions as if I had the authority to do so or that the deceased belonged to me, but I didn't know that Msgr. Vivas was making the same decisions. I felt terrible during the Mass because all people looked very skinny to me. I told my spiritual director about this, and he said, "Pray, so that may go away."

Later, I told Msgr. Vivas, and he told me, "We are skinny because of sin. It is our lack of spiritual life." I thought we were going to starve to death, but Monsignor told me differently. He said we were weak in the spirit and that we should pray much more. Anyhow, I kept on seeing people so skinny.

On August 14, there was the great feast of the Virgin Mary to close the Marian Year. I thought, "Better to stay in my own room than be looking at skinny people."

But Father told me, almost as if giving me an order, "Bernardo, let's go to the procession."

I got on the back of the pickup truck, and we left. We arrived at the new square, where the Holy Father was offended, and I got off along with some boys. [The name of the new square is "19 de julio." This commemorates the date the Sandinistas took power in Nicaragua, July 19, 1979.] Father told me: "No, Bernardo. It is going to be at the Square of the Republic."

That day I did not see skinny people. I walked to the next square along with the crowd and saw that beautifully dressed images were being brought. I thought, "Well, how about Our Lady of Victory Parish? Does it not belong to this diocese, and had nobody invited it? This organizing committee is totally inept, because they should have invited it just as they invited the other ones. Our Lady of Victory Parish is being ignored!"

But then I thought again, "Hey, I am blaming the committee members, and I am also to blame because I should have suggested that Our Lady of Victory should participate in this great demonstration in honor of the Virgin Mary. I would have brought her even on the pickup truck!" So, I calmed down, because at first I had judged the others, but then I saw I was also at fault; I was also to blame. So I quieted down, and at that moment I started hearing a locution again. The Virgin was telling me:

Bernardo, why do you worry that I did not come to this great Marian demonstration? I am here represented under all my titles, and I am very happy. Now, under the title of Our Lady of Victory, I am very busy {this is an expression we Nicaraguans use frequently, "I am very busy"}*before the Lord. I am getting the victory for you before the Lord under this title, and that is why I did not want to come to this demonstration. Because, the days will come when I will go throughout Nicaragua in great processions under the title of Our Lady of Victory. That is why I made the committee members and you forget to invite this parish. Do not get mad at them or at yourself, because this comes from me. I am before the Lord, and when I obtain the victory for you all, then I am going to go out.*

She repeated these words. I was filled with joy, because I was enthralled in this dialogue with her. People in the procession would say, "Hello," to me, and I would answer, "Yes, yes," but I was listening to her and did not want anybody to distract me. They told me, "You look prideful today, Bernardo. You don't even say, "Hello!" But I was in another world; I couldn't tell what I was hearing. The locutions ended near the Tiscapa Lagoon. [This is a famous lagoon in the middle of Managua. The Presidential palace is located next to the lagoon.]

Suddenly, people began to shout: "The Virgin. Look at the Virgin!"

"Come on!" I thought. "Now these people have lost their minds. It is just like it was in Cuapa. They come to see the sun [the phenomena of the sun], and they will not listen to the message."

"They would tell me, "Bernardo, look!" poking my arm. I thought some would fall down, because there were holes in the road.

When we passed in front of the Military Hospital some patients came out in their gowns to look at the procession very respectfully. There were also some nurses and even militiamen. I thought, "Oh, Lord, You are so good! Religion is not practiced in the Military Hospital, but these militiamen still have faith, because they have a prayerful attitude, and they are soldiers and nurses of this hospital! There still is faith!"

But the people continued to disturb my thoughts shouting, "Look at the sun!"

Suddenly I saw that all of the people were raising their hands. I looked up and saw a cloud formation that looked just like a big hand, as if formed by a mysterious sculptor. Toward one side there were three stars forming a triangle, just like the one on the Nicaraguan flag. They were like morning stars, but in the sky there was a very bright sun! "What is this?" I said to myself. "Stars do not shine in the daytime because of the sun, but these ones are shining." It was the midday sun! After that, I went on to the place of the celebration. I attended the Mass, received Holy Communion, and went off rejoicing. That was the locution I received for Nicaragua—the message that she was going to give us the victory and that, when we had obtained the true victory, she was going to go out in processions.

Miriam: Was this at the time of the Sandinista government?

Bernardo: Yes, at that time. When life was the hardest.

[There were until recently plans to erect on one of the hills that dominates the Managua skyline a giant statue of Our Lady of Grace, which was being molded in Italy. It was to be placed upon the same hill that the Sandinista Party had its initials, FSLN. Shortly after the election in February 1990 of Mrs. Chamorro as President of Nicaragua, the Mayor of Managua had the Sandinista's letters torn down, and declared that Nicaragua belonged to the Blessed Mother. The project has been temporarily suspended because of safety concerns. We have heard two different explanations, but both involve different meanings of the word *"mine."* In one version, the project has been held up because of fear of land mines planted on the hill during the Sandinista regime.

The other is that the hill is used to mine gravel that is used for construction, and the hilltop (which has moved in the past) is too unstable to hold the statue of the Blessed Mother because of the extraction of the gravel from the hill.]

9. BERNARDO'S EXPLANATION OF WHY BLESSED MOTHER APPEARED AS A CHILD

Miriam: Why did the Virgin appear to you as an eight-year-old girl in 1980?

Bernardo: Well, what I have thought is that, even though the Church has not emphasized it, September 8 was the Nativity of Our Lady. I understand that the Virgin wants us to know that she was a child just like any other child, simple and humble. Now, in other apparitions, she would present herself as a queen. That is why I say her beauty was natural, because she had no ornaments of any kind. She was as in absolute poverty, but still she was very beautiful. It was the Virgin's birthday, so she wanted to present herself like that.

10. MESSAGE FOR PRESIDENT CHAMORRO

Bernardo: The pastor of the Nindiri parish asked me to give a Marian talk to a group of people from the Legion of Mary. I told him he had to obtain the Bishop's permission, so after he did, I went. This pastor has two parishes to look after, one at Tisma and one at Nindiri. [These two towns are located in the Masaya Department, which is south of Managua.] On Sunday, the 4th of April [1992], I went with him to the Nindiri parish, where people from the entire jurisdiction were going to come in pilgrimage to gather together. Father told me: "These people are going to feel very honored and happy if you go and receive them yourself. So, go and welcome them!"

Very happily I went to receive them and entered the city of Nindiri in a procession going up to the church. In the ceremony, Father sat down and I was at his side watching how the Legionaries made promises to the Virgin, while I waited for my turn to talk. The church was packed!

Suddenly I started hearing the Virgin telling me, *"Bernardo, the Lord is very sad."*

"Why is that?" I thought. I could not speak out because

Father would think I was talking to myself.

Because he has seen the sufferings of his people. Many
collective sins are being committed in Nicaragua by its
government, the ministers and advisors, and by the
people.

"What is this?" I thought. I did not understand the word
"collective sins." I thought collective actions related only to
work, but not that sins might be committed in a collective or
corporate manner.

So you can see the collective sins which are being com-
mitted in Nicaragua, I am going to show them to you.

Then there came a great paper scroll in the air, like an
enormous roll of parchment, and it began to unroll as if
being opened by giant hands. It was the map of Nicaragua,
but you could not see the land, only the two lakes.
Everything else was covered by black and dirty charcoal-like
things. Then great swarms of egg-laying flies came all over
the country. What I was seeing was horrible! She told me:

These are the collective sins which are being committed
in Nicaragua and the entire world. I want this to be
known, so you have to tell about it. People need to
know this so they can change. I want them to change.
Do not keep it to yourself, because it is an urgent mes-
sage. Do not be afraid, for the Lord will help you and I
will protect you.

You know that when you open a roll of parchment and
then you let it go, the two ends will roll back up at once. Not
this one; it closed itself as if somebody was rolling it up
again from one side and then it disappeared. After all this
was over, I went back to the seminary. Father said that I
looked suddenly saddened and quiet. It was not that I was
sad, but that I was meditating about what I had just seen.

On that night, I had dinner with Msgr. Bosco and another
priest, but I did not tell what had happened to me. On the
following day, at the seminary, I did not go out at the second

recess, but stayed alone in the classroom. I was there thinking, when again I heard and saw exactly the same thing as
the day before. So when Father [Santiago Anitua, S.J., at that time
the Dean of the Seminary] came, I did tell him. He immediately
called Monsignor [Bosco Vivas, now Bishop of Leon] and told him
what had happened to me. Monsignor asked me, and I
repeated the whole story again. Then he said, "This is
urgent." Whenever there is a message, Monsignor tells me to
wait a little, but this time he said do it immediately: "Go and
tell. You have to tell!"

Then I began to resist. I did not want to tell about it. I
thought: "How am I going to say this? Who am I to tell this to
Señora Violeta [Barrios de Chamorro, President of Nicaragua]. She is
the President, and she doesn't even look at me anymore! If I
say I want to see her, nobody is going to make an appointment for me!" Tuesday and Wednesday went by. On
Thursday I received the same message once again, but I still
did not tell anyone.

In this I know I allowed the devil to tempt me, for my
reluctance to tell the message was a temptation from the
devil, because he did not want me to spread the message. I
heard the voice of the devil telling me in my inner being:
"Poor Violeta! What are you going to tell her that for! Nothing
will you gain from it! Don't you see that she is sick, and you
are going to offend her? She is a lady, and men have to be
considerate with ladies." He was telling me all of this, and I
felt sorry for her. Around those days Señora Violeta was
requesting that one of Nicaragua's debts be condoned, and I
was thinking about it. "Look at how much the poor woman
worries! What are you going to tell her that for!" And also,
"Remember when you were depicted in those tabloids, the
Semana Cómica [a weekly satirical publication in Nicaragua, no longer
published] that makes fun of everybody, and *La Barricada* [a
then very pro-Sandinista daily newspaper in Nicaragua] where they
ridiculed you with that message of yours {he did not say the
Virgin's message; he will not name her} and you did nothing.
You had to live in hiding during four years. Remember when
they handcuffed you and questioned you. You are going to be
in hiding! You are doing so much good to people, spiritually
and materially. You like to work and always go here and

there, but you are going to face the same plight once again."
He would tell me all of this.

"Oh, my God," I said to myself, "it is Satan himself!" I would take up my rosary and begin to pray. But as soon as I stopped, the attack came back. So I had to keep constantly praying until finally I told Msgr. Bosco.

He told me, "Well, tell the message and pray!"

I had to keep on praying without ceasing! I could not even study my lessons, nor rest. When eating, I would hear the temptations and I could not enjoy my food! I could do nothing, not even have a time of leisure. I had to keep on praying and praying. Then I thought, "They say Father Anitua is a holy man. I have never sought his counsel. He is my teacher, but I have never asked him about these things." So very early I went to the seminary and told him everything I had been experiencing, about the voice of the Virgin, about the map, and about the voice of the devil. Father Anitua would only listen to me.

But before I thought of seeing Father, the devil had told me, "Don't go to see that old man, because he scourges people with a whip!"

The blood of Christ! No one has ever beaten me, not even when I was a boy, and I am horrified when I see children being scourged. But I thought, "Even if he whips me, I will tell Father everything." And I did. He listened to me without saying a word. When I was finished, he told me:

Look, the voice of the Virgin, that comes from God, and also the map and all what she said. But the rest that you heard, that voice that only with praying the Rosary would go away and that would come back when you stopped praying that is the voice of the devil. Now, it is true that when a penitent asks me for penance for his or her sins and wants me to scourge him or her, I do. There is the whip {he shows me a 20-strip braided leather whip} but I respect the will and freedom of the person. If he or she asks me freely, I will do it. But I will not scourge you.

I didn't know that Father would do that to penitents when they asked, but the devil had told me so. The Father gave me the following advice:

> This is what you are to do. The devil tells you half truths. If you meet with government ministers and advisors, they will call the news people, and they are going to make a big fuss about it. To avoid it, we are going to be smart, just like the devil, because he doesn't want the news to be spread. There is the President's secretary. Tell her so she can put it in writing and have copies made, so you can give one to Chico Rosales [Francisco Rosales, Minister of Labor in the Nicaraguan Government] or his wife, and the same day it will get into Señora Violeta's hands.

> That was exactly how it happened.

Then Father told me: "If you hear the voice again, rebuke him and tell him to go present himself at the feet of the crucified Christ." Then he blessed me and gave me some rosaries for the people to pray, telling me that was all he would recommend me to do. I went away relieved as if a great burden had been lifted from me. I felt happy, very happy.

That day I attended class in peace, but in the afternoon, when I was in my room, the devil came back and said to me: "Aha, so you did go to see the old man! You did not heed my words! Now you will suffer the consequences."

Then I did what Father told me to do. I said: "Begone, Satan! Go prostrate yourself at the feet of the crucified Christ! You do not have any power over me, because you are a creature just like me. The one I fear is the Lord God, my Creator!"

I did not hear his voice again, but a varicose ulcer opened up in my leg causing a great erysipelas that attacked me with high fever and shivers. I shook and felt terrible. The fever would go and come back, and my whole body would itch terribly. Also, I came down with a great diarrhea. "Oh, don't let him kill me!" I would pray. I was sick the entire month of May. I missed a whole month of classes, but I could still save the school year, because a seminarian friend of mine would give me his notes.

This is how the message was given directly to government

officials. A relative of the President came and told me: "It is not enough for me that Señora Violeta only received a paper. You yourself would have told her much more nicely. We are going to take you to her house for a private meeting."

So we went and she welcomed us, offered us coffee, and everything was fine. Then I told her the message, and she listened to me very attentively. Then she said to me: "Yes, my boy; everything will be fulfilled. Everything is going to be all right." Then she hugged me and kissed me.

One year later, all the corruption in the government was coming out into the open.

11. MESSAGE TO THE WORLD

Miriam: Bernardo, are there any messages that would apply to the whole world, not only to Nicaragua?

Bernardo: Yes. The message about the collective sins being committed in Nicaragua also applies to the whole world, because it is not only in Nicaragua that collective sins are being committed, because we are all human.

However, in this case the explanation of the messages is a theological one, because as we were discussing with Father [José Bermúdez of the Archdiocese of Washington, who was visiting Bernardo at our house] last night, there is a great deal of tradition and history behind it. The core of the message is a call to prayer, conversion, love. It says, love one another, do your duty, forgive one another, make peace. It also says to serve your neighbor, because this is good in the eyes of the Lord, to serve the needy.

For me, the entire message has great value. Even if it were viewed as insignificant, some people will still be touched by parts of it. And others will comprehend the fullness of the message and be touched deeply by its grandeur.

[Many admirers of Marian apparitions have initially expressed interest in Cuapa and then have (as did the Nicaraguan people for a time) "moved on." Perhaps, they wanted to rush on to the "next show," or as Bernardo would put it, come to see the sun dance and not even listen to (let alone live) the messages. But the simplicity of the Cuapa message is basically the simplicity of Christianity, no matter how clever or complex minds may try to embellish it. As someone has remarked, "the Apostles were not whiz kids." While the Bible and the *Catechism of the Catholic Church* are packed with spiritual truth and insights, it all boils down to the teaching that God is Good, we are wounded, and Satan is bad news. Christ came into the world to give us the help to overcome our weak nature, the false attractions of our community, and the wiles and snares of the evil one. If we trust in Christ, follow His commands, stay loyal to His Church, and—with His Mother, His saints, and His angels assisting and cheering us on—persevere in the race, victory over death lies before us.]

12. MEANING OF "MAKE PEACE!"

Miriam: What did the Virgin mean when she said: *"Make peace"?*

Bernardo: She said, *"Make peace, do not only ask for it."* It is because sometimes we ask, "Lord, give me this," but we don't even try to do our part, to try to understand the other person, and to know how to forgive. This is why she also calls us to dialogue, telling us to talk things over with your husband, with your wife, with your children, with neighbors, so problems can be solved in a peaceful manner. Let me give you an example. One day this lady had a toothache so bad that even her face was swollen, and when you have a bad toothache, you are in a bad mood. A friend of hers came and said, "Hello," to her. She would only answer, "Yes . . . bye," but it was because she was hurting badly. The other lady later commented, "Well! I saw so-and-so and she was mad, she was acting strange." But it was that she had a terrible toothache! Sometimes we think that a friend of ours is mad at us, but it may very well be that he or she has a problem!

That is why the Virgin, as our Counselor, tells us to talk things over with one's husband, daughter, or neighbor, because maybe we don't know what is troubling them inside, what is their suffering, and maybe that is why we see them bitter and sad. You may think they have an attitude toward you, and if you cannot understand, then you have a conflict and you become upset. This way you are not making peace. That is why the Virgin says, *"Do not only ask for peace, but make it, for if you don't make it, there will be no peace."* We also have to cooperate.

13. Meaning of "Active, Diligent, Not Passive"

Miriam: Bernardo, when the boys were sleeping, and you tried to wake one up, and he said, "I'm tired, let me sleep," the Virgin told you: *"I want them active, diligent, not passive."* How do you interpret those words?

Bernardo: Active, diligent, not passive. There is a lot to talk about this. It could be that these boys were good boys, but not qualified for the priesthood. In fact, all of them later dropped out. There was a time when Msgr. Mondragón, who was the dean, would order those who he saw had no vocation to go work with me at Our Lady of Victory. The twelve that at that time were with me later dropped out. Maybe she wanted us to understand that these boys had no priestly vocation; they were good boys, but had no vocation. It could also mean that she wants us to be diligent in fulfilling the duties our Lord has given each one of us, at work and elsewhere, and that we help one another. Because some people are passive, they will not move!

14. Healings at Cuapa

Miriam: Have supernatural healings occurred in Cuapa?

Bernardo: Yes, there have. Señora Julia Guevara was the first person to receive her healing. She was the only sick person at the place of the apparitions. (She had breast cancer.)

Her husband would tell her: "You are crazy. You only go after Bernardo. Did you also lose your mind? Take your medicines . . . !"

But she would reply: "Don't give me that . . . If I die, let me die. I am going to the place of the apparitions," and she would go with me.

During the last apparition, on October 13, 1980, I told her, "Look! The Virgin is there!" But she could see nothing.

She said she looked up, but since she saw nothing, she thought, "Maybe Bernardo has lost his mind!" Then she saw a cloud in the form of a censer, and she thought: "My Lady, I am not worthy of seeing you, but this is enough for me to believe that you are here! There is no fire, nor burning coals, anything, but I see this smoke going up! Anyhow, please heal me!"

After that, she went to check her skin, and it was like a baby's! She had received her healing. She also received another grace from the Blessed Virgin without even asking for it. Her husband would go to the bar, and he would spend the little money they had drinking. That was why she had to start working. Now, after her healing, her husband believed and stopped drinking. Later, both of them would go to church together, until the time he died. That was the first miracle the Virgin did there.

Then there was a nurse. Her son's feet were twisted, and a Cuban doctor told her that he would need an operation at the Military Hospital. The woman was poor because her husband had left her with two children. And the operation would be very expensive. She did not want her child to grow up with defective feet, so she went out to borrow money, but she thought: "I'm going to be in debt and will not be able to repay it." Then she went to Cuapa, to the place of the apparitions. People would get dirt from the ground to take home, so she also took some fine dirt. She made mud and smudged it over the boy's legs and feet and prayed. Then she went to Managua with the borrowed money.

When the doctor examined the boy's feet in order to operate, he came out of the room saying: "What did you do to him, Lady? What doctor saw him? The boy's feet are perfect!"

She said "Nothing. I did nothing." She did not want to tell him about the mud or the prayer because she realized he was not a believer. He was Cuban, one of those internationalist doctors.

Then the boy shouted: "Mommy, the doctor says I am healed! The mud you made and put on me did it!"

"Hey," said the doctor, "your son is telling on you. He says that you put some on him. What kind of dirt is that?"

"Well, it was dirt from Cuapa, the place where the Virgin has appeared!"

The doctor said: "Daughter, take your boy home. He

needs no operation at all!" Then he added, "If there are
things that you have to call miracles, this is one of them."

Miriam: Is the Church keeping a record of all these miracles?

Bernardo: Yes. When there is a doctor treating the sick person and a miracle healing occurs, the records are requested,
including x-rays and doctors' certificates, in order to submit them to the bishop and keep a file of the Virgin's miracles. Then there are the spiritual miracles. I like the
spiritual miracles better, when you see the church full of
people going to confession, and when unmarried couples
who have been living together ask to be married and put
their lives in order.

15. NAMES OF THE VIRGIN

Miriam: When you have seen the Virgin, has she identified
herself with a name other than Virgin of Cuapa?

Bernardo: The Virgin has only one name, which is Mary. We
give her the other names. For example, Our Lady of Lourdes.
She said she was the Immaculate Conception, so her name
should be "Mary of the Immaculate Conception," but people
call her "The Virgin of Lourdes." It is because she appeared
at that place. The same happens with the Virgin of Fatima, in
Portugal. These are names we call her by.

   She is the one and only Blessed Virgin, the Mother of
God. She confirms it saying, *"I am Mary, the Mother of God
and Mother of all sinners,"* as she said in Cuapa. She herself told me when I asked her, "What is your name?" *"My
name is Mary."* She did not say, "Mary of Cuapa." We add
"of Cuapa" because that's where she appeared.

16. TITLE OF THE ANGEL IN DREAM OF JULY 8, 1980

Miriam: When you had the dream with the angel, on July 8,
1980, did the angel have any kind of title? Did he say
whether he was an archangel?

Bernardo: No, he did not use any titles. But when I wanted
to know what his name was, he said: *"I am the guardian of*

the entire American continent." That means that he is the first
guardian of all the custodian angels of the American nations.

17. BIBLICAL REFERENCES

Miriam: Have you had any experiences with visions or locutions about biblical places?

Bernardo: Not about biblical places nor anything related to
the Bible. Sometimes the Lord tells me about things in the
Bible, like the time when He asked me, *"Don't you believe in
the One who made the sun to stop?"* I did not know that, but
it says that during a war the Lord made the sun to stop. When
the Lord told me, *"Elijah was a man just like you and he
asked that it might not rain and it did not rain, and then he
asked that it rain and it did,"* then I thought, "It is true," but I
did have doubts about it until somebody told me where it was
in the Bible [*James* 5:17-18; *1 Kings* 17:1-7; 18:42-45]. But I have not
had locutions about the Bible or about biblical places.

Miriam: Now, about the sun being stopped, in reference to
what did they tell you that?

Bernardo: People would tell me, "You are talking nonsense!
Who can stop the sun? It is not sun that moves, it is the earth!
And if the earth would have stopped, it would have gone out
of its orbit!" But that was what He told me.

One day I was commenting about this with Señora Sarita de
Chamorro, and her husband was nearby reading a book.
"Look," I told the lady, "some people bother me with this idea
that the Lord made the sun to stop. I really don't know, but I
do believe in the Lord. He is the Almighty. It was He who
made the sun and the earth. Why couldn't He make the sun
stop? They are denying the Lord His power, who is All-pow-
erful! [Bernardo's keen observation is often ignored by the technically and
scientifically gifted mind. One of the best, albeit simplistic, arguments that I
have ever heard about the Real Presence of the Body and Blood of Christ
in the Eucharist is: If God can make all of creation out of nothing, what lim-
its His power from making ordinary bread and wine into His flesh and
blood should He choose to do so? And, if He says He has, it must be so,
as He has spoken.]

Her husband came closer to us and said: "You know you're right, Bernardo. The Almighty can do anything He wants with his creatures. I am going to prove it with science."

Then he brought a book published by NASA, where there was an article about a research project to establish what had happened in the very beginning of the world. The article says that the group of scientists used a powerful computer to make calculations. The machine started working, but at a certain moment, it stopped. The researchers exclaimed: "The computer broke down! Let's call the repair people."

The repair technicians said, "The machine is fine!"

They turned it on again, and it got stuck at the same precise point! One of the scientists said: "We are missing one day. The Bible says that the Lord made the sun stop for one day!"

"Come on!" blurted out the other researchers. "You're crazy." And they paid no attention to him. But the computer kept stopping at the same spot. They hurriedly looked for a Bible and found it did not speak of an entire day, but of *"almost one day"* [*Joshua* 10:13].

"It's true!" they shouted. "It is a few minutes and seconds less than a whole day!" They found a way to add the time that was missing, and the computer kept on going until reaching the present time.

"Do you see?" said Señora Sarita's husband. "With science I am showing you that it is true what you're saying, that the Almighty can do anything He wants with His creatures. Of course! It was not the sun which really stopped, but the earth that stopped in its rotation."

"You see?" said I, "then they want to deny the Lord's power."

Fernando Chamorro is the name of the person who has that book in Nicaragua.

18. DREAM WITH ST. JOAN OF ARC IN 1981

Miriam: Has a saint given you locutions or appeared to you?

Bernardo: Not a male saint, but a female saint did appear to me in a dream. At the time I did not know her name, but when I told about it, a Frenchman who came from the same town where St. Joan of Arc was from, he told me it was her. [St. Joan of Arc was born in Domremy (Meuse), France.]

It was a dream, a locution in dreams, announcing to me what would happen with the military service in Nicaragua, where 12-year-old boys would be taken from their homes to be drafted. I had come back to the seminary from Granada, and they told me to go rest because I looked exhausted. I lay down and slept. Then I dreamed that some "IFA" [the brand name of the type of truck that was used by the military to pick up young men and boys to take them to fight in the mountains] trucks were entering the city of Granada, filled with soldiers who would grab 12-year-old boys from their homes and take them away. Msgr. Mondragón's sister, Melba, had two small sons, so she was desperate! The whole city was crying. Only sobs and lamentation were heard from mothers because their children were being taken away. I saw that some of the boys would cry, some others began to talk a lot and still others would become very serious, like little men, as if saying, "Nothing is happening to us." The children had three different reactions. When Father's nephews were being taken away from their mother, she started crying and insulting the soldiers, while her little daughter would cling to her skirt. Melba wanted to hit one of the militiamen, but she was pushed away. Then I told her, "Melba, do not resist. Don't worry. I am going with them."

She leaned against a wall and cried bitterly.

When the trucks came, I got on one of them. One of the soldiers said, "What is this old man coming here for?"

Another commented: "See how he gets on. He can still hold a rifle, so he is fit for combat."

"Yes, I am able," I assured him.

The other one replied, "Well, maybe to peel bananas for the boys' lunches."

I went with them. We were taken near León, to a farm that had been confiscated. I am not against military service nor against physical exercise, as I have already said. What I didn't like is what they told the boys to indoctrinate them, to have them brainwashed, because, they would ask them, "Who is your father?" "This one," the boy had to answer pointing to the rifle. "Who is your mother?" Wham! They would pass the rifle quickly to the other shoulder. "This is my mother." They were denying the boys their parents' love!

They would ask them: "Is there a God?" The boy had to take a rifle, raise it with both hands and respond: "This is god."

As a Catholic, I would die in horror! This way they would instill thousands of mottos, taking away the love for their families, the parents, and everything. They would tell them that kissing or praying to the Virgin were signals of cowardice, that they should be brave and do no religious stuff. This happened every single day!

Then I would tell them: "No! You have to honor your father and your mother. We must be Catholic and commend ourselves in the hands of the Lord. The Lord is good. He is merciful." This is the way I would teach them when the militiamen were not around or were not watching. This indoctrination was something that bothered me a lot, and it was increasing in its intensity, so the boys were getting used to it. I would say, "This is a bad environment. My God, what can I do? Blessed Virgin, please help me!"

In my dream, one day we were in the countryside, when I saw a woman coming among the boys holding a big banner with a cross. She came up to me and gave me the banner and I took it. She did not say anything. She just went away, and I stood there with the banner in my hands. I am going to describe her to you, for it was from this description that I subsequently learned it was St. Joan of Arc. She was a rather short woman, with a strong body and blue eyes. Her skin was white, but tanned by the sun. Her hair was blonde, although it was badly chopped, as if she herself had cut it with scissors. When I received the banner it was facing me, so I turned it around for the boys to see.

"Look at what it says: Praise Jesus and Mary." And very happily they would shout: "Praise Jesus and Mary!"

Then I saw that the militiamen took their bags and left, leaving us alone. So I told the boys: "Boys, the militiamen are gone. We are free! Let's go thank the Virgin, Our Lady, over there in Cuapa! Let's go visit the sanctuary!"

So we went. I was carrying the banner and the boys were shouting: "Praise Jesus and Mary!"

When we got to the old little chapel we prayed the Rosary and again shouted, "Praise Jesus and Mary!"

After that, when we came to the new church, the place of

"The Reclamation" [the place in Cuapa where the Virgin reproached Bernardo, in May 1980, for not having spread the message she had given to him a few days before], and the place of the apparitions, we prayed again. We kept on doing it at every stop. So I told the boys, "We are very happy here, but I am going to give you back to your parents, because they do not know that we are already free." We took the river road and upon crossing the river I felt my feet wet. At that moment, I woke up.

I related the dream to Msgr. Mondragón and told him: "Father, your nephews! There is going to be a persecution against boys." Thereafter, Father sent his two nephews to the United States. When the decision was made to expand the military service, the boys were already here in the States. But there were indeed 12-year-old boys who were taken to war. Once, I want to my hometown, and I found mothers crying because a few boys were in prison. I went to the Human Rights Office, and I published articles in *La Prensa* [a Nicaraguan daily newspaper]. Finally, they delivered the boys to me and we took them from prison.

What I mean to say with this is that my dream with St. Joan of Arc came true. We only had one doubt: "Who was that woman?" asked Monsignor. "Was it the Virgin?"

"No," I replied, "it was not the Virgin. It was another woman. Maybe a saint?"

Some time later there were some Frenchmen who came to conduct an interview. The hometown of one of them was the same as St. Joan of Arc's. When I described the woman I had seen in my dream, he told me: "No direct pictures or images of St. Joan of Arc have been found, except the portraits artists have painted according to the descriptions made by those who knew her. Now, you have made exactly the same description. So, it follows that this woman in your dream must have been St. Joan of Arc."

Later I saw a picture in a book which a lady had to teach children, and I said, "This is the woman I saw." Somebody read the paragraph, and it said it was St. Joan of Arc. This happened in 1981 before military service started. When I had this dream, I was in Managua, because I was hiding from persecution.

19. SEES NO ANGELS WITH BLESSED MOTHER

Miriam: Have you seen the Virgin with the angels?

Bernardo: No. I have seen her in a cloud, utterly beautiful. The last time, she was carrying the Child, when I saw her apparition at Our Lady of Victory. But not with angels.

20. PROBLEMS IN THE CHURCH

Miriam: Has the Virgin spoken about the Catholic Church? For instance, about problems in the Church, the number of Christian churches, the future of the Church or of the Pope, of the Cardinal or the Bishops?

Bernardo: No, not directly. But I think that indirectly she has, because all of us make up the Church—priests, nuns, the religious, and lay people. She talks in general terms to all people, without addressing anybody in particular. What I think is that our Mother wants each one of us, whether a priest, a nun, or a lay person, to look for ways to help, to see that we are doing wrong or right. She spoke in general, but each one has the option to review something that is not going right in his or her life. This is why I say that she had not talked about anybody in particular; the messages are for all.

21. HEAVEN

Miriam: Have you had a dream or apparition where you have seen Heaven or Purgatory or Hell?

Bernardo: Yes, I saw Heaven. When I received the locution on January 20—I can't remember the year though—the Lord told me, *"Look at Heaven!"* Then I saw it. The Lord himself mentioned Heaven, Purgatory, and Hell when He told me that for people for whom everything they would do for the good of others, it counted as a second baptism, they would go to Heaven. Those with less merit go to Purgatory, and then there were the condemned ones. These places were only mentioned by Him. But Heaven I did see. There everything is full of joy, of utter beauty, full of divinity. The Blessed Mother also showed me the four groups of persons in Heaven. [See "The June Dreams with the Blessed Virgin Mary" in Part I.]

22. SATAN

Miriam: Have you ever heard the voice of the devil or an evil spirit?

Bernardo: Yes, when he would tell me not to say anything to Señora Violeta, because I would bother her, and I would end up being locked up and all those other things. When I saw him, he had such enormous black teeth, and he was very, very ugly. I also saw him dressed up as a woman. Once I saw him as an elegantly dressed man who would offer me riches if I would do what he told me. But that was different; there he looked like a businessman.

23. CORRUPTION IN SANDINISTA GOVERNMENT

Miriam: Has Our Lord or the Virgin Mary told you anything about the corruption within the Sandinista government, other than what you have told us about in the message you already mentioned?

Bernardo: Yes, there was a message about the Sandinistas, but I would rather not tell it now, for publication, because people are going to take it in a political context, and that is dangerous. I do not want people to say later that the Cuapa message had political connotations. It is better for it to remain private, until a time when there is a better discernment and explanation of it.

> [In 1981, Bernardo delivered a message to the nine "comandantes" that ruled the Sandinista government. Bernardo does not desire to make this message or related ones public at this time because many of the people involved still hold powerful positions or have friends in high places in Nicaragua.]

24. MESSAGES OF PREPARATION AND HOPE

Miriam: Out of all the apparitions in Cuapa or Our Lady of Victory, which is the one with the biggest impact for you?

Bernardo: The two of them have struck me a great deal, and I feel very happy with both the apparitions and dreams. All of them are so beautiful. Now, about something else. I understand that Cuapa is the place of the preparation. I mean that it is a message about getting ready and working for the liberation of everything.

Notice that the message at Our Lady of Victory Church in El Crucero, is a message of triumph, because it says, *"Burn bad books, books on atheism and communism, and porno-graphic magazines."* Then I thought, "My God, how am I going to do it?" Then I asked, "Isn't it wrong to burn books?"

"Wrong is to burn the sinner!"

But, how can sinners burn? The Virgin warns us not to live in sin, and if we do sin, to get up and start anew. Because what is going to be burned is sin, not sinners. Then she added:

> Do not think that you are going to be burning books all of your life. What I want is to set a symbol, because atheistic communism is going to disappear like smoke into the air from all of Russia and from all over the world.

That is why I say the Cuapa message is a message of preparation. The message in El Crucero at Our Lady of Victory Church is one of hope.

She also says this: *"If you change and convert"*—these are the conditions she requires—*"soon, very soon you will see an end to your sorrows."* There is our hope!

25. IMPENDING PUNISHMENTS

Miriam: Has the Virgin told you anything about impending punishments?

Bernardo: Only when the hurricane was coming, she said there was going to be a punishment, but not in general. It is not that the Lord wants to punish people. We ourselves can see that, as a consequence of our own sins, these disasters occur. I prefer not to say "punishment," because people get gripped by fear, and when they hear the word "punish-ment" they tremble. It is the same as when a father or a mother has to rebuke a son or daughter so he or she may grow up righteous. The same is with the Lord.

[We think Bernardo's caution here is prudent. In many people who closely follow alleged apparitions of the Blessed Mother we see often in some of them a deep, driven desire to learn about "impending punishments." It is unclear to us if they want God to "sock it to them" (others, we presume) or if they want to build a physical preserve somewhere to "ride out the storm." God's punishments, it seems to us, however, have been inherently implanted into our nature and our natural world. Some punishments, just like the rain, fall upon the "good" as well as the "bad." In others the righteous ultimately end up paying the financial and social costs of the wicked in one way or another. If we build our house too close to the water's edge, we should only expect the ravages of the sea or the floods. If we continue to build along earthquake faults, we should expect to be shaken at some point. If we misuse our bodies, why should we not experience the pains of AIDS and various forms of cancer? We live in a world where punishment abounds from sins and "stupidity" of our own as well as others. Most of us, however, never see the constant Hand of God. But such punishment seekers should not be condemned. Even Christ in the last days before His crucifixion had to foretell the destruction of His beloved Jerusalem and weep over it.

We remember driving Bernardo down Pennsylvania Avenue in Washington, D.C., in January 1993, shortly after the new American President announced the pro-abortion, pro-homosexual policies of his infant administration. Bernardo, seeing the impressive federal buildings muttered, "What a pity! So many beautiful buildings!" Miriam immediately asked Bernardo why he said that. Bernardo kept silent.]

26. BERNARDO'S MESSAGE TO AMERICA

Miriam: Our last question. What exhortation could you give the people of America regarding their present moral situation?

Bernardo: I ask all people in America, from the North to the South, to do their best to comply with the Blessed Virgin's message. That is from where our strength to go forward will come. It is a fight we have to fight, because the enemy also wants to take us down a different path. But we, with the help of all of the Blessed Virgin's messages and everything we have received from her, can make it and avoid all the corruption in America. We also have to help other people with prayer, for prayer is the most important thing. If we do not have God, through prayer or through our Blessed Virgin, we are doomed! Our work will bear no fruit! So we have to pray, pray, and keep on praying.

See what happened to us in Nicaragua: We had such a big war, so much blood shed brutally! No liberation was to be found until people started praying. Not everyone prayed, and those who did may not have done it very earnestly, but it was only then that Nicaragua was delivered from communism. There still are some pockets here and there, but it is because we have not done our work right. We have forgotten the Lord! Sometimes not on our own account, but because of the enemy, because we do have an enemy that wants to take us to damnation, and that enemy is Satan. So, this is what we have to do: Pray and let's get to work! Let's get to work for the good of our nations, so parents are able to raise their children uprightly. There are no better teachers than the father and mother in the family. We should not rely only on religious schools or religion teachers for the spiritual growth of our children. The best school is the home, the father and the mother, and even the grandmother. I say the grandmother, because my Granny helped me a lot. I would not have become what I am now without her help. I see I am different from my own brothers and sisters; we love each other and care about each other, but we are not the same.

So this is what I ask: Pray, and insist on the religious education given by parents in the family. This has been grossly neglected. This is what the devil wants to do; he tries to wreak havoc among married couples and Christian families, so everything may be lost! But I know he has been unable to accomplish it.

Well, my warmest greetings and best wishes to America, to all American men and women, and I ask the Lord to bless us and the Blessed Virgin Mary to cover us with her mantle. So be it!

Epilogue

"DREAMS DO COME TRUE"

On August 19, 1995, Bernardo Martinez's boyhood dream became reality. Bernardo became a priest in the line of Melchizedek, a priest of the Holy Roman Catholic Church. The following report was prepared by Miriam who attended both the ordination and first Mass of "Bernardo of Cuapa."

Bernardo's Ordination

On Saturday, August 19, 1995, over twenty priests, nearly 50 seminarians, and 500 of the faithful from all over Nicaragua crowded into the historical and beautiful Cathedral of Leon, the Basilica of the Assumption, built in 1747, to witness the ordination of Bernardo Martinez, humble Nicaraguan peasant, chosen visionary of the Blessed Virgin Mary, and faithful, obedient, and loyal son of the Holy Roman Catholic Church.

The Cathedral was brilliant in its appearance. Pink roses abounded. The altar was covered by a white cloth which protruded over the front of the altar. Embroidered on the side facing the congregation in big letters was "Ave Maria." In the front right corner of the sacristy, elevated above the heads of all, stood a life-size statue of the Blessed Mother. Adorning this beautiful statue were pink roses and a sign which said in Spanish:

105

Bernardo, hijo mio:
¿Qué no estoy yo aqui,
que soy tu Madre?
[which translates to English as:]
Bernardo, my son:
Am I not here for,
am I not your Mother?

No visible indication was evident of any fear that might have been caused as the result of thirteen bombings or attempted bombings in recent months of Catholic churches or schools in Nicaragua. In fact, during the week prior to the ordination, Bishop Bosco Vivas, the Bishop of Leon, was in the Cathedral praying the Rosary near midnight one night. He heard a strange noise and left to call the police. The police arrived and captured an individual who was attempting to place a bomb in the Cathedral. Diabolical forces exist in Nicaragua that are angry with the Catholic Church for its constant effort to prod whatever Nicaraguan government exists to protect the rights of the poor while respecting the rights of God.

Bishop Bosco Vivas officiated in an awe inspiring ceremony, filled with love and many tears of joy. During the ceremony, Bishop Vivas told the congregation:

I consider that Deacon Bernardo has a vocation to the priestly ministry because he spent several years receiving training in the Seminary and because I know he has a spirit of an apostle, of dedication to God, and of service to others.

Regarding the Lady of Cuapa's message, the Bishop added:

It is an invitation to love and forgiveness, to prayer and the fulfillment of everyone's duty, and to a contemplation of the mysteries of the Holy Rosary . . . . It is also an invitation to ask the Lord in faith in order to be able to face adversity, to attain repentance, and to live the Christian life.

At the conclusion of the ceremony, now Padre Bernardo Martinez mounted the pulpit and made the following remarks:

> I want to thank Bishop Bosco Vivas, who was very understanding with me. It was through his understanding heart that I am here today. Also, I want to thank the priests with whom I worked at the Seminary and in various parishes in Managua. I give thanks to all of the people who have been united in prayer with Jesus on my behalf, because I am a fruit of Our Lord Jesus Christ's prayer, and of the prayers of all the priests whose help I requested so many times. I also want to thank all the persons who gave me material help to defray some of my training expenses. Thank you all for all your help. Here is your priest. I am yours, and here I am for you.

At which point, Padre Bernardo ended his remarks as thunderous applause filled the Cathedral.

Following the ceremony, Padre Bernardo was greeted by most of those in attendance who came forward to touch his hands, ask for his blessing, give him a hug, present a gift. All sectors of Nicaraguan society came forward: the rich, the poor; the powerful, the weak; the old, the young; male and female. With constant spontaneous singing in the background, tears of joy continued to fill the Cathedral during this touching period of personal thanks that lasted for over an hour.

Afterward, Bishop Vivas hosted a reception for Padre Bernardo which was attended by many who came to the ordination. Among those present were Sister Paula Hildalgo, one of Bernardo's longest and dearest friends, and several supporters from the United States who have befriended the Church in Nicaragua and Bishop Vivas and Padre Bernardo in particular.

Padre Bernardo's First Mass

On Sunday, August 20, 1995, while the front page of the newspaper *La Prensa,* Nicaragua's leading newspaper, declared "Bernardo of Cuapa Ordained Priest," Padre

Bernardo returned to Cuapa, Nicaragua, his home town and site of the 1980 apparitions of the Blessed Virgin Mary. It was his 64th birthday and the Feast of St. Bernard of Clairvaux after whom Bernardo was christened.

Padre Bernardo was led through the streets of Cuapa by a procession of the local people who were singing joyfully. The procession ended at the new chapel in Cuapa where he would celebrate his first Mass. Inside the chapel was the statue of the Blessed Virgin Mary which first illuminated in April 1980, the statue which Bernardo fell in love with as a young child. The statue was dressed in a new, beautiful blue gown. It was now contained in a niche protected by a heavy glass door as a result of precautions taken after the October 1993 vandalism of the chapel which resulted in the smashing of one statue of the Blessed Virgin Mary and breaking into the tabernacle and desecration of the conse- crated hosts. An overflow crowd from Cuapa and other cities and towns in Nicaragua filled the chapel. The people were excited and happy to greet and see "their priest."

After the Mass, Bernardo made a few remarks. Shortly after beginning, the heavens showed their abundance by a thunderous downpour of rain. The downpour was so exten- sive that people who came to the Mass and wanted to visit the site of the 1980 apparitions with Padre Bernardo were unable to do so because the runoff made the stream that must be forded to reach the apparition site impassable. The downpour also delayed all the visitors to Cuapa when they headed home as they had to wait until the Las Lajitas River, at a location which is about 20 kilometers from Cuapa, stopped overflowing the only bridge that provided access for vehicular traffic.

In his remarks, Padre Bernardo offered timely advice per- taining to the evangelization of today's youth:

> Brothers and sisters: Something that is of great con- cern to me is the raising of children. We live in a very difficult world, a world that binds young people and children with strong chains in this twentieth century. This grieves me profoundly.
> Those of you who are parents and godparents, and

even grandmothers, you have to take extremely good care of your children. Please train them well! Teach them to pray, just like my grandmother taught me to pray, caring for the fruit that the Lord has chosen. The fruit was chosen by the Lord, but it was my grandmother with her prayers, sacrifices, advice, and encouragement who educated me so that I could finally get to stand here on this occasion—so very important to me. Therefore, my brothers, I want all of us—parents, godparents, and grandmothers—to do this: Teach our children to pray. I know I learned the Rosary from my grandmother. This is what grandmothers should do, teach their grandchildren to pray the Rosary to the Blessed Virgin, Our Mother, and to pray to Jesus in the Blessed Sacrament.

I remember when I used to come to church with Granny and, after Mass, she would make me kiss the floor because Jesus, in the person of His representative on earth, had been there to celebrate the Holy Sacrifice of the Mass. We used to spend hours in prayer.

Well, I do not want this seed to go to waste. I want it given to the children, boys and girls, because that is where priests come from. They come from families where parents teach their children how to pray. Do not teach them the horrible songs that sometimes they play on the radio! Don't listen to that! Turn the radio off and forsake those things, because technology may be used to lead us to Heaven, but also it can lead us to Hell. It depends on how we use it! So, if we use the radio to listen to the Rosary when it is being prayed, or a talk on a Christian subject, then we are making good use of the technology or science that man has received from God. Unfortunately, sometimes we do not use it for good purposes.

This is why I say to parents to be very careful with their children. Do not allow them too much freedom, either! Do not allow them too much freedom, because if I had been raised in a profligate manner, with no respect for or belief in religion, that seed through which God had chosen me from before I was born—

because, as Jeremiah says, the Lord also knew me from before—that seed would have been lost. It would have fallen by the roadside, where it was trampled by everyone, even run over by cars. It would have fallen on hard ground where it dried up. But, through my grandmother's help, the seed was well cared for, and the ground wherein it fell was good. It may have been late, but for God it is never late because for God there is no time. It is all as one day for the Lord. Therefore, my brothers, I want you to do this and ask for the Lord's help to do so.

My grandmother helped me even in my afflictions and my sufferings. When I was hurting and crying, she would comfort me, singing songs to me. She taught me to pray to Mary our Helper saying:

It is Mary our Helper, sweet lighthouse of the sea.
Since I first learned to love, the love of my soul is she.
Each of my childhood steps she did guide,
And for that, since childhood, my love for her abides.

My grandmother used to teach me that. She knew many songs and prayers by heart. Maybe a little old lady would say, "But I can't read." However, surely she knows some prayers by heart. My grandmother couldn't read either!

When I was especially troubled and sad, she would teach me a song that goes like this:

Some wander the earth in search of happiness,
but not those like I who already possess it;
It flourishes in my heart, not like a wilting flower,
but like an early-blooming rose of perpetual spring.

When I was greatly distressed and sorrowful, and I did not want to work at all, she would comfort me with these songs.

This is what you should do also, those of you who are parents and godparents, because godfather means father and godmother means mother, so you too are fathers and mothers. And also the grandmother.

With these holy memories and with a great joy in my heart, I say to you all: So long and, again, thank you very much!

After Mass, there was a reception for Bernardo given by the local people. Constantly smiling, he graciously accepted the heartfelt thanks and best wishes of his many friends and neighbors. August 19 and 20, 1995, were two electrifying days for those who had the opportunity to share in Bernardo's dream. They will never be forgotten.

Padre Bernardo is currently stationed in the Diocese of Leon as the pastor of the parish of Our Lady of Perpetual Help in Tonalá, a small, malaria prone, village that is located northeast of Leon near the boarder with Honduras. Consistent with his past practices, Padre Bernardo has already started construction on a permanent church for the village. After a recent pastoral visit by Bishop Bosco Vivas, Bishop Vivas reported on how impressed he was by the number of people participating in the worship services and the faith and devotion among the parishioners in Padre Bernardo's parish.

Appendix

Selected Prayers for the Americas

"Hear, O Lord, the cry of Your people," proclaims the psalmist. But is the Lord hearing such cries coming from the Americas? And if so, among the billion inhabitants, how strong is the signal He is receiving? The Blessed Virgin Mary, when greeting her cousin, Elizabeth, cried out *"And His mercy is from generation unto generations that fear Him."* Do we in the Americas "fear" the Lord? Do we wonder in awe at His majesty, His glory, His power, His justice, His mercy?

Personal communication with God is called "prayer." Prayer is to the Christian soul what breath is to the body. It is the raising of one's heart and mind to God. It is also speaking with God. Prayer is not a monologue but a dialogue, a conversation. The four general types of prayer are adoration, thanksgiving, contrition, and petition. There are differences between liturgical or public prayer and private or personal prayer. When praying as part of the collective Church, we must say the words and prayers as proscribed by the Church. Freelancing, no matter how creative, is not appropriate for the laity or the clergy. However, in private prayer we can be creative, we can use any words, book, posture, or time of day that helps us develop our conversation with God. We have to develop good habits of prayer. Formulas followed as a youngster no longer are sufficient for the adult mind. At first, we must make time for prayer and remove ourselves from the "rat race" of modern society. As our prayer life grows, we look forward each day to those precious moments with our God. In prayer lies the beginning of peace in the world, peace within our own beings, peace with our spouses, our children, our relatives, our neighbors—and peace with God. As the Blessed Mother says, *"Without God there can be no peace!"*

Without daily prayer our spiritual heart does not pump at a level to make us fully vibrant. It produces only a comatose condition. And, of course, without any prayer, our soul is dead, hardened, closed, decaying, etc.

But why does one sense there is so little prayer in the Americas, and, in particular, in the United States? The daily spiritual meditations in the *Vatican II Weekday Missal* contain these insights:

(Difficulties in Praying)—Why do some followers of the Lord let their prayer life dry up and atrophy? What happens to bring about the hardening of the spiritual arteries? Here are some of the problems with prayer in our times.

112

A serious problem is created by electronics. The person who starts his day with the radio is ill prepared for any morning prayers or mediation. The person who watches TV for six hours a day, or who watches the late programs, will be so fragmented intellectually as to be incapable of quality prayer. The youngster whose nervous system throbs to beat music cannot relax enough to pray. In order to pray you need silence and peace of soul. You have to control electronic noise.

The excuse that one is too busy is given by many who do not pray. But it is an excuse. The Lord Jesus, after hard work all day long, habitually went out at night into the desert to pray. It is a matter of personal priorities. The fact is that people do not pray for some other reason—and then say they are too busy. Not one of us is too busy to develop a good prayer life.

Why do Christians not pray? One reason is a lack of organization. A healthy prayer life means regularly—even when we don't feel like praying. Prayer is ordinarily work. The lazy person who does only what he or she likes to do will pray only once in a blue moon. And the person who prays only when in the mood will find months, even years, going by without any praying. The individual who is always late, never organized, never neat—that individual will never be much at praying. St. John of the Cross wrote about people who had fat in their souls and could not pray—an idea inaccurate in biology but accurate in spirituality. Discipline is necessary for prayer, as for anything worthwhile in this life (1303-04).

There follows a selection of prayers, some of which have been adapted to reflect the messages given to Padre Bernardo. The reader who prays little is encouraged to look them over. Feel free to modify any private prayer (of course, in a theologically sound manner) to reflect your own situation, your own problems, your own concerns—your own personal crosses you must carry each day.

Some people like to share their pain with others. Others often like to say that they share the other's pain. Both are needed. Each day we must share our pains with the Lord. But we, through contemplation and remembrance of the wounds suffered during the Passion and Crucifixion of Jesus Christ, must always be aware of the suffering we personally have caused God through our own sins of commission and omission.

These prayers are offered for personal use only and not as formal liturgical prayer.

Remember, *"Prayer is the answer!"*

Prayers For Private Use Only

1. Prayer Before a Crucifix

Look down upon me good and gentle Jesus, while before Thy face I humbly kneel and, with burning soul, pray and beseech Thee to fix in my heart lively sentiments of faith, hope, and charity, true contrition for my sins, and a firm purpose of amendment, while I contemplate with great love and tender pity Thy Holy Wounds, pondering over them within me and calling to mind the words which David Thy prophet said of Thee, my Jesus: *"They have pierced My Hands and Feet, they have numbered all My Bones."*

For the intentions of the Holy Father, the Vicar of Christ:

In remembrance of the hundreds of Holy Wounds to the Prince of Peace and the Suffering Servant caused by the scourging at the pillar, the crowning of thorns, and the fallings down—O Brother Jesus, forget us not for we are sinners. *(Say three times.)*

In remembrance of the Holy Shoulder Wound of Christ caused by carrying the Cross for our sins—O my Jesus, forgive us our sins, save us from the fires of Hell, lead all souls to Heaven, especially those who have most need of Your Mercy.

In remembrance of the Holy Wounds to the Feet of the Good Shepherd and the One Who walked on water—Our Father, Who art in Heaven, . . .

In remembrance of the Holy Wounds to the Hands that healed and broke bread—Hail Mary, full of grace, . . .

In remembrance of the Holy Wound to the Side of the Sacred Heart of Jesus from which His Merciful Graces and Most Precious Blood flow upon us sinners—Glory be to the Father, . . .

2. Prayer to the Holy Spirit for the Americas

Come, Holy Spirit, cover the Americas with Your Love.

O Holy Spirit, purify our minds, so corrupted by so many false philosophies which permeate our culture, some of which are just a modern twist of an ancient error. Help us find truth amidst the fog that surrounds us.

O Holy Spirit, mend our hearts. Where they have unjustly hardened against any person, race, or nation, soften them. Where they are too soft, toughen them. Where they have been bruised or broken by violence, abuse, hate, or indifference, heal them. Fill us with hope so we do not despair.

O Holy Spirit, open our eyes to the reality of eternity, to the existence of Heaven and Hell. Give us the grace to choose good over evil, light over darkness, and life over death.

O Holy Spirit, cleanse our ears so we may hear the guidance You have written on our consciences, and that we may understand and follow the teachings of Your prophets and Jesus Christ as handed down to us throughout the ages by the Holy Catholic Church, which is constantly under Your protective wings, and which is headed on this earth by the Vicar of Christ, the Holy Father, our Pope, and those bishops in union with him.

O Holy Spirit, comfort us, purify us, mend us. Constantly bestow Your graces upon us so that we may love life, cherish life, and defend life. Set us on fire so that we may help You renew the face of the Americas.

3. Personal litany to the Blessed Virgin Mary for the 21st Century in the Americas

Lord, have mercy on the human family.
Lord, have mercy on the human family.
Christ, have mercy on all families in the Americas.
Christ, have mercy on all families in the Americas.
Lord, have mercy on our families.
Lord, have mercy on our families.
Christ, hear us.
Christ, graciously hear us.
God, the Father Almighty, Creator of Heaven and earth, Sustainer of our existence, Knower of all things, our Abba,
Have mercy on us.
God, the Son, Eternal Word, Prince of Peace, Lord of Lords, King of Kings, Suffering Servant, Redeemer of the world, Savior of mankind, as our Brother Jesus, like us in all things but sin.
Forgive us.
God, the Holy Spirit, Wonderful Counselor, Breath of Life, the Paraclete, Sanctifier of the world, Inspirer of prophets, Motivator of peacemakers, our Advocate,
Set us on fire so we may help You renew the face of the earth.
Holy Trinity, One God, Holy God, Holy Mighty One, Holy Immortal One, Holy Awesome One, Holy Merciful One; Father, Son, and Holy Spirit, a sacred mystery of Love,
Rain down Your Grace upon us.

Holy Mary,
Pray for us.
Holy Mary, Mother of God,
Pray for us.
Holy Mary, Virgin most powerful,
Pray for us.

Holy Mary, Virgin most beautiful,
Pray for us.
Holy Mary, Virgin most truthful,
Pray for us.
Holy Mary, Virgin of virgins,
Pray for us.

Mother of our Savior,
Pray for us.
Mother of our Redeemer,
Pray for us.
Mother of the Church,
Pray for us.
Mother of God's people,
Pray for us.
Mother of a pilgrim people,
Pray for us.
Mother of all Christians,
Pray for us.
Mother of the homeless,
Pray for us.
Mother of the poor,
Pray for us.
Mother of our benefactors,
Pray for us.
Mother of the new creation,
Pray for us.
Mother of the repentant,
Pray for us.
Mother of reconciliation,
Pray for us.
Mother of the dying,
Pray for us.
Mother of Sorrows,
Pray for us.
Mother of Divine Grace,
Pray for us.
Mother of Good Counsel,
Pray for us.
Mother of the Way,
Pray for us.
Mother of the Truth,
Pray for us.
Mother of the Life,
Pray for us.
Mother of the Light,
Pray for us.
Mother of our Hope,
Pray for us.
Mary, immaculately conceived
without Original Sin,
Pray for us.
Mary, as at Cana,

our intercessor,
Pray for us.
Mary, since the foot of the Cross,
our spiritual mother,
Pray for us.
Mary, assumed body and soul
into Heaven,
Pray for us.
Mary most pure, model for
clergy and religious,
Pray for us.
Mary most chaste, model for
the single life,
Pray for us.
Mary most loyal, model for
married couples,
Pray for us.
Mary most giving, model for
all women,
Pray for us.
Mary most caring, model for
pregnant women,
Pray for us.
Mary most loving, model for
all parents,
Pray for us.
Mary most joyful, model
for youth,
Pray for us.
Mary most faithful, model
for the laity,
Pray for us.
Handmaid of the Lord,
Pray for us.
Guardian of unborn children,
Pray for us.
Refuge of sinners,
Pray for us.
Sanctuary for the addicted,
Pray for us.
Comforter of the afflicted,
Pray for us.
Health of the sick,
Pray for us.
Help of all Christians,
Pray for us.

Cause of our joy,
Pray for us.
Tower of David,
Pray for us.
Temple of the Holy Spirit,
Pray for us.
Ark of the new covenant,
Pray for us.
House of gold,
Pray for us.
Mystical rose,
Pray for us.
Star of the sea,
Pray for us.
Gate of redemption,
Pray for us.
Gateway of Heaven,
Pray for us.
Mirror of justice,
Pray for us.
Seat of wisdom,
Pray for us.
Vessel of honor,
Pray for us.
Highway to Jesus,
Pray for us.
Queen of the most Holy Rosary,
Pray for us.
Queen of the Holy Family
and our families,
Pray for us.
Queen of Saint Joseph and all
Christian husbands,
Pray for us.
Queen of integrity,
Pray for us.
Queen of modesty,
Pray for us.
Queen of chastity,
Pray for us.
Queen of purity,
Pray for us.
Queen of patience,
Pray for us.
Queen of kindness,
Pray for us.

Queen of humility,
Pray for us.
Queen of justice,
Pray for us.
Queen of mercy,
Pray for us.
Queen of peace,
Pray for us.
Queen of patriarchs and prophets,
Pray for us.
Queen of confessors, virgins,
and martyrs,
Pray for us.
Queen of the apostles and
their loyal successors,
Pray for us.
Queen of all the disciples of
Jesus Christ,
Pray for us.
Queen of the holy angels,
Pray for us.
Queen of all the saints,
Pray for us.
Queen of the universe,
Pray for us.
Queen of Heaven,
Pray for us.
Favorite Daughter of God
the Father,
Let us experience your faith.
Mother of the Son of God,
Let us share in your hope.
Sacred Spouse of God the
Holy Spirit,
Let us magnify your charity.
O Holy and Mystical Mother,
Cover us with your mantle.
Lamb of God, You take away the
sins of the world;
Spare us, O Lord.
Lamb of God, You take away the
sins of the world;
Graciously hear us, O Lord.
Lamb of God, You take away the
sins of the world;
Have mercy on us.

Let us pray:

O Heavenly Father, we pray that through the intercession of the Blessed Virgin Mary, we may be preserved from all danger of sin and led to everlasting joyful life with You, now and forever. We ask that You will grant us the grace to become more like our Holy Mother in our daily lives. We ask this in the name of Jesus Christ, Your Son, Who lives and reigns with You and the Holy Spirit, One God, forever and ever. Amen.

4. O Holy Mother, Rescue Us!

O Holy Mother, you came to the Americas in the year 1531 at Guadalupe to tell your demoralized sons and daughters that you were their Mother and that they should end their pagan practice of human sacrifice. In doing so, you brought to your new sons and daughters faith in Jesus Christ, hope in eternal life, and an awareness that, because God loves each of us, we should likewise love each other.

Today many of us in the Americas no longer have that faith, that hope, that love. The faith of our past has been mocked as our elderly are killed through euthanasia. Some have lost hope for the future as mothers are encouraged to kill their babies through abortion. Many have even despaired of giving or receiving any love in the present as an individual's right to commit suicide garners acceptability in our cultural subconscious. Very few, perhaps only a small remnant, sense the future disasters we are imposing upon ourselves unless we change.

Life, the priceless gift from our Heavenly Father, has become cheap as God is divorced from our daily lives. The family, the natural community created by God to mirror His image and the relationship that exists among the Holy Trinity, and motherhood itself, are under attack by diabolical forces.

O Holy Mother, you know only so well the conditions we have brought upon ourselves. We are helpless to stem the tide by our own efforts. Please ask Jesus Christ, your Son and our Brother, to send the Holy Spirit upon each of us to energize, invigorate, and enliven us. Have the Holy Spirit remove from our eyes, our ears, our minds, and our hearts whatever blocks us from understanding the eternal truths ordained by God. Ask your Son to send the Holy Spirit to purify our arms and our legs, our lips and our tongues, our eyes and our ears, our minds and our hearts, and our souls and our wills, so that we can see, can understand, can accept, and can do God's Holy Will. We plead for your assistance, O Holy Mother. Please do not abandon us for are you not our Mother? Amen.

5. Prayer for My Family

Heavenly Father, most good and gracious God, sustain my family in Your love. Make it a place where holiness can abound. Help us to learn to be like Jesus in all our actions. Aid my family to imitate the Holy Family of Jesus, Mary, and Joseph. Help us to learn from the good example of others while likewise giving good example. Assist us in learning to bear our pain and suffering as Jesus did. Aid us in overcoming the difficulties in carrying our crosses. Help my family life to lead only to Jesus, the source of true happiness. Please give wholesome, holy habits to my family.

Dear Lord, watch over all the young people in my family. Open their hearts to Jesus and His call to faith and life in the Holy Catholic Church. Help them to be courageous and responsible in all their actions so that they can become more like Jesus. Preserve them from the seductions of the senses to which they are so vulnerable. Give them a deep respect for other people and their rights.

Dear Lord, help each member of my family to put away desire for material things which distract us from You and Your life with us. Give us a love for the poor and less fortunate. Make us always eager to serve those in need. Please aid us to grow in knowledge of the truth, in holiness, in goodness, and in that life which we hope to share with You forever in Heaven. Amen.

6. Prayer for Difficult Children

Lord Jesus Christ, as the perfect model for all men and women, You understand the pressures upon today's young people. The options and opportunities open to all people today are more extensive than at any time in history, but the demands and moral dangers for all of us are also greater.

I am concerned especially for these young people in my family: *(name the children who are having moral difficulty)*. They seem angry at us and morally confused much of the time; terribly selfish and self-centered; rebelling against authority; rejecting us, Christian values, and religion; and scorning the support and love of their family for their own ways.

Help me to be patient through this trying time. Keep me from criticizing my children, comparing them to others, expecting them to give more than they can or be what they are not. Help me resist giving in to any demand which will harm them permanently, and let me allow them freedom to decide those things they safely can.

I turn my concern for these children over to You and Your Mother, Mary. May You and Mother Mary restore their balance and give them a sense of holy purpose. May You guide them to a right pathway and give them the courage and confidence to take those first steps. Amen.

7. Father's Prayer to St. Joseph

O St. Joseph, whose protection is so great, so strong, so prompt before the throne of God, we Christian fathers place in you all our interests and desires. As God the Father entrusted His Son into your care, our Heavenly Father has likewise entrusted us with the souls and well-being of our children. Help us to love our own spouses as you loved Mother Mary. Give us the courage and the wisdom to protect, defend, and cherish our spouses and children.

O St. Joseph, you were active and diligent, not passive, in protecting Jesus and Mary. You taught, nurtured, and watched Jesus grow. You lifted the child Jesus up into the air, and He laughed and smiled His love for you. We lifted Him up on the Cross, and He lovingly forgives us. O St. Joseph, help us to be active and diligent with our families.

O St. Joseph, just as God the Father, Jesus Christ, the Holy Spirit, and the Virgin Mary trusted you, we trust you also and ask you to please assist us by your powerful intercession before the Holy Trinity, and obtain for us all the spiritual blessings we need through your Divine Son, Jesus Christ, our Lord and our Brother.

O St. Joseph, we never weary of contemplating the infant Jesus asleep in your arms. We dare not approach while He reposes near your heart. Press Him in our names and kiss His fine head for us, and ask Him to return the kiss to each of us as we draw our dying breaths.

O St. Joseph, Patron of departing souls, Pray for us. Amen.

8. Private daily Litany to St. Joseph

Lord, have mercy on the human family.
Lord, have mercy on the human family.
Christ, have mercy on all families in the Americas.
Christ, have mercy on all families in the Americas.
Lord, have mercy on our families.
Lord, have mercy on our families.
Christ, hear us.
Christ, graciously hear us.
God, the Father Almighty, Creator of Heaven and earth, Sustainer of our existence, Knower of all things, our Abba,
Have mercy on us.
God, the Son, Eternal Word, Prince of Peace, Lord of lords, King of kings, Suffering Servant, Redeemer of the world, Savior of mankind, as our Brother Jesus, like us in all things but sin,
Forgive us.
God, the Holy Spirit, Wonderful Counselor, Breath of Life, Paraclete, Sanctifier of the world, Inspirer of prophets, Motivator of peacemakers,
Set us on fire so we may help You renew the face of the earth.
Holy Trinity, One God, Holy God, Holy Mighty One, Holy Immortal One, Holy Awesome One, Holy Merciful One; Father, Son, and Holy Spirit, a sacred mystery of Love,
Rain down Your Grace upon us.

St. Joseph, chosen by God the Father to protect His only Son, our
Brother Jesus,
Pray for us.
St. Joseph, chaste spouse of the Blessed Virgin Mary, our
spiritual Mother,
Pray for us.
St. Joseph, vicar father of Jesus Christ, our Lord and Savior,
Pray for us.
St. Joseph, protector of all Christian children,
Pray for us.
St. Joseph, defender of all Christian spouses,
Pray for us.
St. Joseph, guardian of all Christian families,
Pray for us.
St. Joseph, model of fatherhood for all Christian men,
Pray for us.
St. Joseph, model of the holy worker for all people of God,
Pray for us.
St. Joseph, comforter of the poor, the lonely, the outcast,
and the refugee,
Pray for us.
St. Joseph, protector of the One, Holy, Catholic, and Apostolic Church,
Pray for us.
Lamb of God, You take away the sins of the world;
Spare us, O Lord.
Lamb of God, You take away the sins of the world;
Graciously hear us, O Lord.
Lamb of God, You take away the sins of the world;
Have mercy on us.

Let us pray:

O Heavenly Father, we pray that through the intercession of the
Blessed Virgin Mary and St. Joseph, we may be preserved from
all danger of sin and led to everlasting joyful life with You, now
and forever. We ask that You will grant us the grace to become
more like our holy Mother and St. Joseph in our daily lives. We
ask this in the name of Jesus Christ, Your Son, Who lives and
reigns with You and the Holy Spirit, One God, forever and ever.
Amen.

9. Expanded Prayer to St. Michael the Archangel

O St. Michael, send forth your angels to guard our premises at
(specify the addresses of our home/s and business/es, if any).

O St. Michael, send forth battalions of your purifying angels constantly to remove all evil spirits from *(name the places of employment of
you and members of your family)*, the Supreme Court and all inferior

courts of the United States, the Congress, and the White House. Capture and cast forever these evil spirits into Hell. Remove these spirits from all the places and objects and all the people that work in these institutions. Ask them to surrender their evil spirits, and, if, in your wisdom, they continue to refuse to relinquish their evil spirits, remove such persons from their positions and fill the positions with God's people, so that these institutions become instruments to bring God's mercy, compassion, love, and justice into this vale of tears.

Let us Pray:

O St. Michael the Archangel, defend us in battle. Be our protection against the wickedness and snares of the devil. May God rebuke him, we humbly pray; and do thou, O Prince of the Heavenly Host, by the power of God, thrust into Hell, Satan and all evil spirits who wander through the world seeking the ruin of souls. Amen.

10. Prayer for Priests

Sacred Heart of Jesus, hear my humble prayer on behalf of Your priests, especially *(name)* and *(name)*. I pray for Your faithful and fervent priests, for Your unfaithful and tepid priests, for Your priests who labor at home and abroad, for Your tempted priests, for Your lonely and desolate priests, for those You are calling to be Your future priests, for Your young priests, for Your dying priests, and for the souls of Your priests in Purgatory.

Merciful Heart of Jesus, remembering that these men are but weak and frail human beings, give them a deep faith, a bright and firm hope, and a burning love. I ask that, in their loneliness, you comfort them; in their sorrow, You strengthen them; in their frustrations, You show them that it is through suffering that the soul is purified.

Loving Heart of Jesus, keep them close to Your Sacred Heart and bless them abundantly, in time and in eternity. Amen.

11. Daily Prayer for the Priests and Religious of My Diocese

O Holy Mary, Mother of Mercy and Queen of Peace, please keep all the priests and religious of the *(specify the [arch]diocese where you live)* diocese constantly under the protection of your heavenly mantle.

Protect our bishop, our priests, our deacons, our seminarians, our nuns, our brothers, our monks, our postulants, our novices. Draw them closer to the Sacred Heart of Jesus. Guard them from all evils; strengthen their weaknesses; give them hope and wisdom; help them to become more holy; send angels to comfort them, console them, to lead them. Let them shine as bright as the stars to help guide our path through this vale of tears.

Bless them, O Holy Mother, and inspire them. Help them to lead us to holiness so that we can better know, love, and serve God in this world and share eternal life with Him and His Heavenly Hosts. Amen.

12. Prayer for Padre Bernardo Martinez

Our Lady of Cuapa, you and your Son—the Prince of Peace, the Lord of lords, the King of kings, the Suffering Servant—have chosen Padre Bernardo Martinez to be a light for the Nicaraguan people.

To shine:
—as a bulb at the end of a tunnel for those caught in the depths of despair and doubt;
—as a lighthouse beacon for those who are tossed by the storms of life; and
—as a guiding star for those on the path to glory.

Mother Mary, through the graces of your Son, Jesus Christ, bless Padre Bernardo Martinez in his spiritual growth and his evangelization efforts. Help him to become a holy priest, a Eucharistic priest, a Marian priest. Let him become a heavenly example for his fellow priests. Let him bring many Nicaraguans to love and experience the peace of your Son's Sacred Heart and your Immaculate Heart. Guard him. Protect him. Sanctify him.

With the intercession of St. Bernard of Clairvaux, for this we pray.

13. Election Prayer

Lord Jesus Christ, You told us to give to Caesar what belongs to Caesar, and to God what belongs to God. Have we done so? Enlighten the minds of the people of the Americas, now more than 500 years after the discovery of the new world by Christopher Columbus. Have we chosen a President and other government officials for our nation according to Your Divine Will? If not, O Lord, have pity on us. Give our citizens the courage always to choose leaders for our nation who respect the sanctity of unborn human life, the sanctity of marriage, the sanctity of marital relations, the sanctity of the family, and the sanctity of aging. Grant us the wisdom to give You, what belongs to You, our God. If we do this, as a nation, we are confident You will give us an abundance of Your blessings. Amen.

14. A Closing to Private Prayer

Heavenly Father, protect the *(specify your country or nationality)* people, and keep them loyal to Your Son, to His Holy Catholic Church, and to His Blessed Mother. Bless the shepherds of these people with the graces necessary to practice the virtues required to lead them to the City of God, the heavenly Jerusalem. Bless *(name the president or leading public figure of your country)*, and fill him/her with Your graces, and give him/her an extra dose of patience. Bless the nuns at *(name a group of contemplative nuns)* and all the other people around the world that pray for the souls of the faithful departed. Purify those souls and cleanse their robes.

Have compassion on the innocent victims of the violence, hatred, abuse, indifference, and greed that permeates the world. Inflict the wrath of Your justice upon those who willfully, intentionally, or know-ingly inflict such injuries. Bring awareness to those who inadvertently cause such injuries so that they may abate what they are doing, rectify the harm they have caused, and atone for the injuries that have been suffered.

Protect all of Your visionaries around the world. Protect the village of Medjugorje and the parish of St. James. Protect and sanctify the priests that have served at St. James, are presently serving at St. James, and who will serve at St. James in the future.

Bless the Americas and give them a renewal, a new Pentecost, a spiritual awakening. Send forth Your Holy Spirit, Your angels, Your saints, and the Blessed Mother upon the Americas. Let a new birth of Your kingdom reign in each person from pole to pole and shore to shore.

Lord, let us see Your holiness in Your creation, in Your Church, in Your priests, and in Your people. Let us see this holiness so that we become humble, and in becoming humble we lose our pride.

Heavenly Father, saturate us with Your blessings of modesty, chastity, and purity. Give us the graces to love life, cherish life, and defend life. Give us also the graces to "Be not afraid," to help the poor, to comfort the sick and lonely, to correct the errant, to protect the inno-cent, and to proclaim the Truth!

For Your honor and glory; yesterday, today, and forevermore! Amen.

Faith Publishing Company

Faith Publishing Company has been organized as a service for the publishing and distribution of materials that reflect Christian values, and in particular the teachings of the Catholic Church.

It is dedicated to publication of only those materials that reflect such values.

Faith Publishing Company also publishes books for The Riehle Foundation. The Foundation is a non-profit, tax-exempt producer and distributor of Catholic books and materials worldwide, and also supplies hospital and prison ministries, churches and mission organizations.

For more information on the publications of Faith Publishing Company, contact:

Faith Publishing Company

P.O. BOX 237
MILFORD, OHIO 45150
U.S.A.

THE
RIEHLE
FOUNDATION...

The Riehle Foundation is a non-profit, tax-exempt, charitable organization that exists to produce and/or distribute Catholic material to anyone, anywhere.

The Foundation is dedicated to the Mother of God and her role in the salvation of mankind. We believe that this role has not diminished in our time, but, on the contrary has become all the more apparent in this the era of Mary as recognized by Pope John Paul II, whom we strongly support.

During the past nine years the Foundation has distributed books, films, rosaries, bibles, etc. to individuals, parishes, and organizations all over the world. Additionally, the Foundation sends materials to missions and parishes in a dozen foreign countries.

Donations forwarded to The Riehle Foundation for the materials distributed provide our sole support. We appreciate your assistance, and request your prayers.

IN THE SERVICE OF JESUS AND MARY
All for the honor and glory of God!

The Riehle Foundation
P.O. Box 7
Milford, OH 45150
U.S.A.